TRUE LEADERS DELIVER

With Best Regards,

Peter Cosgrove

TRUE LEADERS

Peter Corijn

OWL PRESS

LEADERS

An essential guide to mission success

DELIVER

*'The thoughts of others
Were light and fleeting,
Of lovers' meeting
Or luck or fame.
Mine were of trouble,
And mine were steady;
So I was ready
When trouble came.'*

*A.E. Housman
(English poet, 1859 – 1936)*

*'Never walk away from home
Ahead of your axe and sword.
You can't feel a battle in your bones
Or foresee a fight.'*

*The Hámavál
(Viking 'Words of the High One', i.e., Odin)*

*A rare book that convincingly explains what leaders must do –
and then clearly shows how to do it. In* True Leaders Deliver
*Peter Corijn, both an experienced leader and brilliant storyteller,
captivates, inspires, and teaches things that are invaluable
to all organizations, and those who must lead them.*

STANLEY McCHRYSTAL
General, US Army (Retired) and Founder & CEO of McChrystal Group

True Leaders Deliver *is a unique book. It's a kit with clear 'how
to' advice and practical tools. Any organization should implement
them, starting today. I know Peter well, having worked with him
for many years during my time as CEO of P&G. I vividly remember
that he was at the same time a disciplined leader and unconventional
thinker, with a breadth of interests. The book benefits from that
trait. It's highly entertaining because a vast canvas of cases and
stories are shared. I for one never thought that I had lessons to receive
from the likes of Alice Cooper and U2. Highly recommended!*

ROBERT A. McDONALD
8th Secretary of the Department of Veterans Affairs, Retired
Chairman, President & CEO of The Procter & Gamble
Company, Chairman West Point Association of Graduates

*Every CEO should distribute this book to all leadership ranks,
from junior to senior. The book's an incredibly rich source of
tools and insights on how to deliver. It contains what every
business leader should know - and more importantly – do.*

PAUL POLMAN
Business leader, campaigner, and co-author of *Net Positive*

I agree with the premise that leaders need an intrinsic drive coming from a will to make a positive contribution for all stakeholders. This intrinsic drive makes them deliver. What sets this book apart is that it provides a leader with the necessary tools and actionable advice on how to make things happen. It does not stop at the insights and strategic level and the tools and advice are based on hard earned experience. It's an engaging read because of clear, compelling cases and the variety of the sources. Strongly recommended.

JEF COLRUYT
Chairman and CEO of Colruyt Group

Prepare to be amused and scared, inspired and challenged. Peter's book is a delightful combination of focused rigor and captivating storytelling, drawn from extensive research, driven by intense curiosity. You will find yourself smiling at the lessons learned from Pablo Escobar's business model, and cringing with embarrassment at the work you will realize you, and your company, are not doing.

ANDREW ROBERTSON
President & CEO, BBDO Worldwide

There are strategy books, execution books, and leadership books. Rarely do you come across one that combines all three. Peter Corijn has written a book that combines research-based frameworks, entertaining examples, memorable quotes, and home-spun wisdom. As a one-stop-shop for how to navigate modern strategy and leadership, True Leaders Deliver *delivers.*

MICHAEL WADE
IMD Business School Professor of Innovation and Strategy
and Cisco Chair in Digital Business Transformation

Wow, what a wise, engaging, insightful, and practical read this was – a rare combination that emerged from Peter's unique business experience and profound curiosity. It was a pleasure to step into Peter's thinking and extract valuable insights, several of which I'll be using to strengthen delivery of my Leading & Living Innovation university course.

JOHN METSELAAR
Professor Innovation at Solvay Business School (ULB), Head of Economy, Strategy & Finance Center at The Conference Board Europe, Retired P&G Innovation Leader.

This business book rocks hard! It brings to mind the renowned SAS Survival Handbook, but with a focus on business. It certainly demonstrates that challenging situations can be conquered, and one can flourish despite crises. With a diverse range of sources and a touch of maverick spirit, Peter provides a wealth of knowledge that should be immediately applied to your business or organization the minute you finish the book. Your team and stakeholders – not to mention your career – will thank you for it.

DIMITRI PANAYOTOPOULOS
Retired Vice Chairman of Global Business Units of the Procter & Gamble Company, Senior Advisor at Boston Consulting Group, and various Board Positions

I love the gung-ho style and wide scholarship – and unlike most business books this one is NOT boring even to an outsider like myself. The Moroccan adventure is really fascinating and is worth the price of the book itself. I have always wondered – how do you turn a company around? Well, now I know, and for the first time I sense the real hard and specific work needed to do that!

ROBERT TWIGGER
Explorer and bestselling author of 15 books, translated in 16 languages, including *Angry White Pyjamas* and *Red Nile*

True Leaders Deliver is exactly what the title promises. Tools based on hard-earned hands-on experience are offered to make a mission happen. It also has that quality too seldom found in business books: it's highly engaging and readable. Peter taps into a wide variety of sources. Insights are drawn from business cases but equally from special forces, history and even from rock stars. Importantly, the advice is always brought back to practice and how to win in the marketplace. It's the sort of book I wish I had read at the start of my career, though senior executives will benefit from it as well. Don't miss it.

TONY SALDANHA
President Transformant, Co-Founder Inixia Inc., Bestselling author of *Why Digital Transformations Fail*

This is exactly the business book my entire leadership team needs. More than yet another book with lots of theory, it's an incredibly rich source of real-life advice on how to sustainably win in the marketplace. Peter manages to back-up insights with useful tools and compelling cases from all walks of life. Everything is put together into one integrated and compelling process, the Lean Organism Model. *Can't wait to get my hands on 100 copies straight away.*

FRANCISCO JAVIER VAN ENGELEN
Board Member & CFO Signify

Peter Corijn was a legendary out-of-the-box creative thinker in his time in P&G. This outstanding book is a continuation of Peter's unique perspective and the discontinuous angles he views subjects. It's a refreshing view that is certain to strengthen the depth of any leader, in any facet of life.

JAMES MICHAEL LAFFERTY
CEO Fine Hygienic Holding

In the evermore dynamic business world, where new, unique, and privileged insight is increasingly powerful and leverageable, Peter's body of work blazes a new trail with fresh perspective that would benefit businesses in any stage of development, from start-up to steady state. A must-read for ambitious enterprises everywhere.

STEVEN P. STANBROOK
NED Imperial Brands, Past COO International Markets SC Johnson

True Leaders Deliver *is a valuable business book for both seasoned leaders and executives and people managing their first team. The book offers a practical road map for leading an organization through strategy, building capability and execution. I have known Peter for many years, he is a successful leader with a proven track record. We are fortunate to learn from his practical experiences and many inspiring examples.*

STEPHEN SCHUELER
CEO of Enerjen Capital, Chairman of European Maritime

There are so many business books out there. Many are interesting to read but not relevant, quite a few are relevant but not interesting to read. Peter's book delivers on both: relevancy and style. It provides deep insights into the concept and philosophy of leadership and, at the same time, translates those into practical, hands-on "how to" tips. Clearly, worth reading and applying.

WERNER GEISSLER
Retired Vice-Chairman of the Procter & Gamble Company

As CEO and author, I've formulated the (IQ+EQ+TechQuotient+BloodyQuick)^{CreativityQuotient} equation as the way towards Peak Performance. True Leaders Deliver *is an outstanding example of bringing this theory to life and weaponizing it through inspirational stories and ready to use tools. Peter is a Master in all five elements. He shares his secrets compellingly in this book.*

KEVIN ROBERTS[CNZM]
Former Chairman/CEO of Saatchi & Saatchi Worldwide, Author of best-sellers *Lovemarks* and *64 Shots*, Founder of Red Rose Consulting

Drawing on examples and experiences from P&G, the military, and the music industry, Peter has developed a management system called the Lean Organism. *It enables you to supercharge your team and drive mission success. Warmly recommended and highly actionable. If you want to play with the best, then learn from the best.*

BRAM DESMET
CEO Solventure, Assistant Professor Vlerick Business School and Peking University, author of *Supply Chain Strategy and Financial Metrics*

Business books are not quite my thing, but every rule has its exception. True Leaders Deliver *completely captivated me. I've kept on nodding my head in agreement with its content. Peter is a great storyteller drawing hard core business lessons from the unlikeliest of sources. If you read one business book this year, make it this one.*

CLAUDE L. MEYER
Retired President of The Procter & Gamble Company

Peter wrote a very insightful, no nonsense, captivating book combining exciting leadership experience, human insights and stories from history. The book is a condensed piece of must-know information for leaders and entrepreneurs. It reads like a novel and is anything but boring (I find so many leadership books boring!). **True Leaders Deliver** *is a very well-written piece of storytelling for those who want to make a difference.*

OLIVIER ONGHENA-'t HOOFT
Executive Chair Global Inspiration & Noble Purpose Institute (GINPI), entrepreneur and solutionist. Author of the acclaimed 'Book of Noble Purpose'

CONTENTS

WHEN EVERYTHING'S ON THE LINE: THE 4 PILLARS OF MISSION SUCCESS & THE LEAN ORGANISM 19

PILLAR 1: THE MISSION SUCCESS EQUATION 29

A. Strategic Clarity 31
    Chapter 1: A Meltdown Requiring a New Strategy 31
    Chapter 2: Essential Prework Before the Strategy Review & Some Reflections on Pablo Escobar's Profit Model 41
    Chapter 3: The Issue with Killing an Opponent and Nine More Considerations When Developing Strategy 49
    Chapter 4: 'From Darkness to Light' – Tools Used, Strategic Choices, and Outcome at P&G Morocco 75
    Chapter 5: Do Trees Look Taller When the Grass is Cut? Defining Go-to-Market Models 82
    Chapter 6: 'The Power of One Dollar' to Drive Strategic Clarity in the Organization 91

B. Perfect Execution 97
    Chapter 7: Lessons from Alice Cooper, Napoleon and Hannibal 97
    Chapter 8: 'Do You Want Teddy Bears or Top Pilots?' Practical Ways to Improve Execution 111

C. Capabilities 121
    Chapter 9
    Learning Plans, Microbattles & Why Leaders Must
        Be Readers 121

D. No Excuse Ownership 135
    Chapter 10
    The Ownership Matrix & The Circle of Influence 135

E. A Hard-Won Iron Man Victory to Summarize the
    Mission Success Equation 143

PILLAR 2: F.A.Y.U.R. 149

F: Fluid Strategy And Execution:
    The Russian Winter 151

A: Agility: Jesters Are no Fools 167

Y: Your Leadership: The Harder Right 179

U: Understanding: Know Your Bubbles 187

R: Resilience: Join the Never Give Up Club 193

PILLAR 3: CHANGE MANAGEMENT 219

A. Why Do We Need Change Management?
    Sex & The Red Queen 221

B. When To Change?
    What Bowie and U2 Got Right 223

C. How to Change? What if the Lord Doesn't Strike
   You Down? 231

PILLAR 4: CREATE A SUPERCHARGED TEAM **257**

PULLING IT ALL TOGETHER IN ONE MODEL:
THE LEAN ORGANISM MANAGEMENT MODEL **273**

Acknowledgments 279

Notes on Sources 281

Selected Bibliography 287

Index 293

WHEN EVERYTHING'S ON THE LINE

THE 4 PILLARS OF MISSION SUCCESS & THE LEAN ORGANISM

Leadership is a complex and multi-faceted topic, but its essence can be distilled into a simple truth: *leaders deliver.* They get things done and leave the businesses, organizations, and communities they serve, in a better state than they found them.

This practical guide is designed to help you accomplish these outcomes and is suitable for both seasoned executives and those new to the business field. What sets it apart is that it provides guidance not only on WHAT needs to be done, but also on HOW to put those recommendations into action. Through a unique combination of insights and case studies from business, history, psychology, Special Forces and even rock stars, it will equip you with the tools needed to take your business and leadership to the next level.

The book will explore the four pillars that serve as the foundation of mission success. A varied set of narratives will successively cover The Mission Success Equation, the F.A.Y.U.R. methodology, Change Management, and the importance of creating a Supercharged Team. Finally, all these concepts will be integrated into 'The Lean Organism Management Model'.

Let's define the core elements of the first pillar with a thought-provoking query: what if your family's lives were at stake? That was the exact circumstance people encountered on June 3, 2017. On that fateful day, a van deliberately rammed into pedestrians on London Bridge. It then crashed on the south bank of the River Thames. The three occupants of the vehicle jumped out and ran to the nearby Borough Market area. The assailants initiated a stabbing spree, with one of the terrorists storming into a restaurant brandishing a large blade. If you were present, what would you do? What resources do you wish you had? The following bullet points are critical, and they also apply to your business:

- **Strategic Clarity:** the mission is 'save my family'. How? Escape. If no other choice, fight back.
- **Perfect Execution:** a clear plan that can be flawlessly executed because all have trained for such an eventuality.
- **Capabilities:** mastery of Krav Maga – the celebrated Israeli self-defence technique – would be a good skill set to have. Knowledge and experience would be at a premium. Merely having the awareness to never wear flip flops outside of the home might already make a difference, because mobility and speed could prove essential.
- **No Excuse Ownership:** This element tops them all; will other people help you? They might but most will focus on running away faster than you. There's a reason why

we admire heroes and stand in awe of recipients of the Medal of Honor: it's exceedingly rare. It's up to you first and foremost. If there's no ownership, all is lost. You alone stand between victory or loss. Failure is not an option.

Rest assured that somewhere on the planet, there is a company working with the mindset 'as if their family was at stake'. This was the case for Elon Musk and his SpaceX team when they tried to get their first rockets off the ground.* Such leaders and companies will beat you unless you act alike. Here's the equation:

Pillar 1: The Mission Success Equation ('MSE')
= (Strategic Clarity + Perfect Execution + Capabilities) x No Excuse Ownership.

However, it is not enough. To get back to the terrorist attack: it's useless to say, 'Boy, I wish I knew karate,' just before the knife hits. It's too late now. Therefore:

Pillar 2: Skills must be built before a crisis happens. A crisis will happen. We just do not know the timing and shape of it.

Let's take a lesson from evolution. It's often said that the species that survives is the one most adaptable to change. There is a key piece missing in that statement: to survive in the face of change, the trait that allows you to thrive in a different environment must already be present in the population.

Here's an example that illustrates the idea: a population of foxes all have short-hair furs, perfectly adapted to the mild

---

* In his first start-up, Musk told an investor: 'My mentality is that of a samurai. I would rather commit 'seppuku' (ritual suicide) than fail.'[1]

climate region where they live. One day, by random mutation, a fox is born with a massive fur coat. Some of its offspring are also much hairier because the genetic mutation is hereditary. The same applies to the next generations. Then, the climate starts to change. It gets much colder. The shorter-hair foxes start to feel mightily uncomfortable. Their offspring eventually freeze to death. Only the longer-haired foxes survive and reproduce, until eventually a thick fur becomes the observed norm. The fox as a species was able to cope with the climate change but only because the feature suited to the new habitat existed in the skulk.

Equally, organizations and leaders must develop the right DNA upfront to be able to overcome future challenges. Evolution happens at random. Organizations need to be deliberate about preparation, and deploy F.A.Y.U.R. The acronym represents:
- **F**luid Strategy and Execution
- **A**gility
- **Y**our Leadership
- **U**nderstanding
- **R**esilience

There's overlap between this and the MSE (see figure 1 on the following page). Indeed, it's hard to get Strategic Clarity and to know which Capabilities are needed without Understanding. Perfect Execution requires Resilience and Agility. Simply everything revolves around Your Leadership.

Unfortunately, there is no such thing as a permanent competitive advantage, which introduces the third pillar.

Pillar 3: We must master change; ideally even drive it to create new advantages in the endless cycle of creative destruction.

'The Red Queen effect' erodes business superiority. This character from Lewis Caroll's *Through the Looking Glass* (the sequel to *Alice in Wonderland*) is running to stand still. The Red Queen is a metaphor to describe that time always diminishes advantage. Unless we progress, we go backwards. To use the words of biologist Matt Ridley: 'Every invention sooner or later leads to a counter-invention. Every success contains the seeds of its own overthrow. Every hegemony comes to an end.'[2] At some point in the future, there will be major disruptions – Black Swans* – that turn everything upside down. History is full of improbable events 'that can never happen'. The world is becoming ever more VUCA (Volatile Uncertain Complex Ambiguous), to the extent that some argue it should be referred to as BANI (Brittle Anxious Nonlinear Incomprehensible). Just in the period 2015 -2023, Europe has faced a mass immigration crisis, global climate concerns, the Covid-19 pandemic, an energy crisis and the impact of the war in Ukraine. Technology, artificial intelligence ('AI'), and digital systems are uprooting many markets and have altered the game. Change Management is a process which we'll discuss in detail.

The final pillar is about ensuring that the entire organization takes responsibility for managing everything that has been covered so far.

---

* The Black Swan tag is given to events that are outliers, with an extreme impact, and with retrospective (but not prospective) predictability. For a long time, Europeans were convinced that swans could only be white. The evidence before their eyes confirmed the thesis. That is, until the discovery of Australia where black swans do exist. One single observation was enough to change the paradigm.[3]

Pillar 4: Create a Supercharged Team that works in sync towards the objective.

Let's flash back to June 3, 2017. Imagine the terrorist had stumbled upon a superbly trained, highly motivated team that moved as one towards neutralizing the threat. That's the kind of spirit you want in your Supercharged Team. There must be so much electricity in the air when you walk around the office that you can charge your phone on it.

Let's add a sobering caveat though to this exalted vision: people are not your biggest asset; the RIGHT people are. Choosing the 'who' for the mission is as important as the 'what' and the 'how' to get there.

That thought completes the 4 pillars we'll develop in depth. You may not need all of them to the same degree, depending on how your business and organization are doing. Figure 1 provides the complete picture. Success sits in the bullseye where all core concepts meet. The whole is bigger than the individual parts.

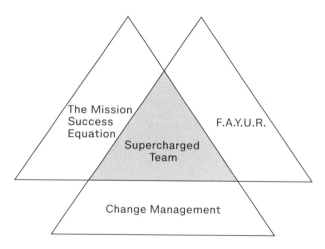

Figure 1: The Mission Success Equation (© Peter Corijn 2023)

At the end of the book, a management model will be proposed that integrates everything. Here's the blueprint of it in figure 2. Don't worry about it for now. Just like on the front of a Lego packaging, I merely want to show you what we will end up building. We will first discuss each brick of each pillar and then fit it all together in The Lean Organism Management Model.

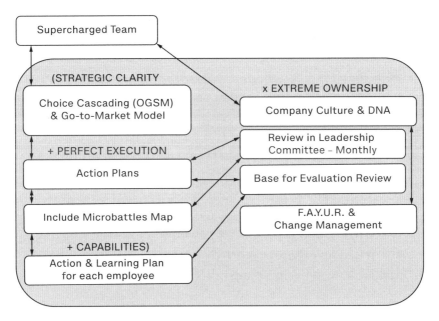

Figure 2: The Lean Organism Management Model™
(© 2017 Peter Corijn / VUCASTAR)

The roadmap of this book:

There are four key sections, reflecting each of the pillars, with one last chapter pulling it all together. Since Supercharged Team is overlapped by the other concepts, much will already have been addressed before we get to that topic. Hence, I will just highlight some extra insights. The core learnings are always highlighted in **bold** font. Those less interested in a topic, or pressed for time, can just read these, and move on. An executive summary is offered at the end of each chapter.

An important warning: sometimes countries or organizations you don't like will be discussed. It's not done for political reasons. My only interest is sharing best practice; no matter where it comes from. You may for instance not be a fan of the Israeli Airforce, but friend and foe agree that they are the best. Some of their tools are hence useful to copy. Anyway, it's smart to learn from competition (or your enemy).

I'm a fan of both analogical thinking and hands-on knowledge. Valuable management lessons can be drawn from a wide range of sources. Humanity is endlessly fascinating in all its endeavours. Inevitably, my executive background and leadership philosophy are part of the DNA of this book. This is my truth, and it might not be yours. However, much is also based on extensive research and interviews with CEOs and leaders, in business and other walks of life.

As much as possible, first-hand experience is reflected. Some examples: to be able to talk about the race to the South Pole, I manhauled on the ice of Spitsbergen with polar explorer Dixie Dansercour. Training for weeks in anti-terror and urban combat with experienced commandos and SWAT teams generated insights on how to plan and execute missions. To understand their concept of ownership, I've participated in programs run by (ex-) Navy SEALs. West Point TLDG and a seminar with General (ret.) McChrystal shed further light on how to deal with VUCA. I've played support act to U2 and many others. I'm a recording indie artist (check out 'Paul Numi' on Spotify) which allowed me to get insights into the music industry. And so forth.

> One case from Procter & Gamble ('P&G'), set in Morocco, will be discussed in extenso. It will be a *fil rouge*. It's hence advisable to go through the details. The case is an integral part of the narrative. A gray line on the left-hand side of the page will serve as a visual indicator throughout the book.

P&G has been fabulously successful for nearly two centuries. It's rightfully one of the most admired companies in the world. I never loved a company more. Still, as you will discover, things can go very wrong in a subsidiary. I chose the P&G Morocco experience because we often learn more from a tough challenge than from an easy task comfortably sailing in the breeze. A captain who has not navigated through a storm is not fully qualified. The same applies to a business leader. There's the risk that some feathers might be ruffled by choosing such a case. But I believe it ultimately shows P&G at its very best.

PILLAR 1

THE MISSION SUCCESS EQUATION

(Strategic Clarity + Perfect Execution + Capabilities) × No Excuse Ownership

A.
STRATEGIC CLARITY

We will first review the P&G Morocco case before delving into the next five chapters, which comprehensively cover all aspects of achieving strategic clarity.

CHAPTER 1

A Meltdown Requiring a New Strategy

'It's a career cemetery.' As that was the third person to tell me since the announcement, I started to get a bit worried. Early 2001, I had just been promoted to run P&G Morocco. After two weeks on the job, it became clear that there was something seriously amiss. I was in for a baptism by fire. Although the business forecast predicted a significant profit, it was not grounded in reality. The forecast relied on the assumption that the last quarter of the fiscal year would ship a much higher volume compared to the same period in the previous year, despite a 10% decline in the first three quarters (a forecast model affectionately known as 'the hockeystick'). Based on realistic trends, the company was headed towards a loss.

Receivables showed considerable issues as well. The bad debt ran into the millions, because of overly generous credit terms in the past. Corrections to the commercial policy had been made but the monies were yet to be written off. In 1999, serious internal control ('IC') problems shook the organization badly. Controls were still weak in 2001 and Morocco was on the global IC watch list. The two local P&G plants were considered amongst the worst in the world. Infrastructure was run down. The state of things was decidedly 'off' because P&G only operated by the highest possible standards, at times generating internal critique of 'why everything always had to be gold-plated' (and hence expensive).

Product quality and customer service were poor. On store shelves, one out of two products had defects. Quality audits rated the plants at -20%, whereas the global minimum threshold was 85%. Typically, production cost was 30 to 65% higher versus Eastern Europe. P&G Morocco had overinvested in capacity and only used about 35% of it. Half of customer orders were incorrectly delivered by product supply and required corrective back orders. Plant safety was a serious concern as well, with incidents having taken place in the past that resulted in physical harm.

The P&G Portfolio:

Tide laundry detergent was the key brand, accounting for 57% of total volume in fiscal year ('FY') 98/99. Yet by FY 01/02, the brand had lost 50% of its volume and no less than 30% share points. Consumers kept complaining about insufficient suds (foam) and harshness on hands. The brand used to be *the* lovemark in Morocco. Now it had turned into a hatemark, with many house managers vowing to never ever buy Tide again. Unfortunately, P&G Morocco was a one profit leg business, with Tide accounting for nearly 100% of the profit. Other brands lost money or made little. Therefore, when Tide collapsed, so did the entire profit.

At the time of the start of this case, there had been months of internal debate between Marketing and R&D about what exactly was wrong with Tide. Rather predictably, marketeers blamed the formula, R&D stated that the marketing was subpar.

A bit of background on the wonderful world of soap is required. Suds are an essential visual signal of cleaning power for consumers who wash clothes by hand. Those of you who still clean dishes in the sink have certainly experienced the same. We also like lots of rich suds in our bath foam. No suds creates the perception that the product stopped working (it's not true by the way). Tide only played in the hand-wash laundry category, where 90% of the Moroccan laundry business was.

There was also a machine-wash laundry segment. It was small because few families could afford washing machines. These detergents have a 'low suds' formula. In an appliance, too much foam creates problems. These consumers have close to no tangible contact with the product. Hence, they do not need the same visual cues and obviously, the effect on hands is of no concern. Premium priced Ariel was offered in both machine- and hand-wash powder. The brand was successful in the former category. It was not doing well within hand-wash because, like Tide, Ariel was rated a harsh product with poor suds. The brand also suffered from some positioning issues.

To make matters worse, key competitor Unilever took the lead in launching polybags on their Omo hand-wash detergent, and eventually scored a major success. Polybags (detergent packed in a plastic bag instead of a carton box) were priced 15% cheaper than cartons. A price disadvantage in the ultra-competitive detergent market equates to a kiss of death. P&G had been late to follow Omo's polybag lead because the profitability on cartons was higher versus polybags. P&G relied on Tide's cartons' profit to subsidize other brands. Polybags were eventually introduced but the packaging had major quality problems and tore easily. The critical wholesale trade segment was reluctant to carry them. One torn polybag per case wiped out their entire profit margin.

Hair Care was not in good shape either. Lack of initiatives and the absence of strong equity marketing had eroded the market share from a high of 30% volume share to 26% by December 2002. Pampers & Always had volume market shares of 90% in very small markets. Most consumers still used cotton cloth, i.e. traditional products. Both brands were expensive and sold at a 50% higher price per unit versus what P&G Poland charged.

Ace was successful within the branded bleach product category. Unfortunately, 80% of the market was in bulk sales force was solid but highly unionized and expensive. After the acquisition, the union had successfully negotiated the same salary curves and benefits as P&G. These were higher than what a typical local distributor would pay.

There was also a General Office site in Casablanca. In total, there were 740 employees, of which 428 were in the plants.

Some of the best-rated employees left. Regretted loss was at a high 20% in 1999. Predictably, there were zero resignations amongst the poorest-rated people. Typically, the worst underperformers were parked in non-jobs, such as doing 'something' in the warehouse. Because of union strength, few were ever fired.

The organization used to pride itself for being a net exporter of talent. In 2001, even some entry level management jobs required expatriates. Judgment was all too often the yardstick for decision-making. Initiative success was only 10%. Morale was understandably low. Most employees were junior. 60% of managers had less than 18 months' experience. Investment in people development was close to zero. Both plants, Comunivers and the General Office had low productivity.

General Office: revenue/employee comparison:

Morocco	Egypt	Balkans	Turkey
100	250	260	233

Note that any restructuring required major effort. It would be a key distraction for management and organization alike. It would impact the ability to bring the business back. The risk of strike was 50/50 (two weeks, possibly longer). On the positive side, a secret project had already been started to investigate rightsizing the organization, codenamed 'Simba'.

The trade:

The trade was traditional, dominated by 120,000 high frequency stores ('HFS', 'mom & pop stores'). The product flow was complex: most HFS were supplied via a chain of wholesalers. It typically took six months for a product upgrade to reach a distribution of 80% of consumption. Some shelves were clogged with 'old' Tide packs because FIFO (first in, first out) was not religiously followed. These old packs had poor quality and were certain to disappoint consumers. Removing them cost up to $3m, money we didn't have.

Rural consumers bought weekly at 'souks' (traveling open markets) or at a small shop in the village. Generally, males visited the souk, not females. The 'modern' trade was not very developed. French chain Auchan operated a local joint venture ('Marjane') and was 6% of P&G's business.

The landscape:

His Majesty King Mohamed VI had taken over the throne mid 1999, backed by a strong desire for change in the country. Economic reforms such as privatization of state companies had been launched. Importantly, free trade agreements had been signed with the Arab League Nations, with the European Community and several individual Arab countries. These called for customs duty reductions on both raw materials and finished products. Each year, duties would be significantly reduced until their planned disappearance by 2012.

P&G signed an investment agreement with the Moroccan government in 2000. The company committed to an amount of capital investment and job creation over the course of five years. In return, the government granted important duty reductions on Pampers' machinery, raw materials, and infrastructure incentives. A meeting was held between Mr. John E. Pepper (Chairman) and the King to celebrate the event. This was very well covered in the national media as a piece of positive news for the development of the Moroccan economy. As a result, P&G had a very good relationship with key Ministers and the Royal Court.

Before the government reforms kicked in, the economic picture was rather bleak. In 2000, GDP went down due to a bad harvest attributed to poor rainfall. The sector was only 15% of GDP but employed >40% of the population. GDP per capita was at $1,500 (for reference, the USA today is around $63,000). 72% of the population were DE class and made less than $250 per month. AB class consumers were highly sophisticated and 'culturally' linked to France. 45% of the population lived in rural, small villages ('douars') with an average of 60 households. Douars were very hard to reach and could often not even be found on a map. Literacy rate was 49% (today 79%). Urban unemployment was at least 20%.

The social climate was tense. Unions were powerful and often called for strikes in case negotiations were not going their way. The labour law was not up to date and not entirely clear on some issues. A major company just went bankrupt after a six months sit-in. This event sent shockwaves through both the industry and the political world. The media tended to support workers and gave high coverage to strikes.

There was one major upside. An HR audit showed that there was tremendous talent in the organization. Recruiting standards had never been lowered. There were lots of great young people, out of which a formidable team would emerge. Turning the subsidiary around would prove the most intense business experience of my life (so far).

I'm sure you're convinced that a change in strategy was advisable. That incidentally is one of the big advantages of a crisis. Nearly all employees will acknowledge that change is required. Let's bring P&G Morocco back, starting with the strategy and hop on *'the Marrakesh Express'* (Crosby, Stills & Nash). But first things first: prework.

CHAPTER 2

Essential Prework Before the Strategy Review & Some Reflections on Pablo Escobar's Profit Model

Strategy reviews require solid prework. Here's a non-exhaustive prework list with an application to the P&G Morocco case. A thorough review of the analysis' outcome has the advantage of getting everybody in the executive team on the same page and to synergize the knowledge prior to the strategy discussion.

1. **Assess the landscape.**
   - What are trends in our industry?
   - What disruption can we expect? What disruption can we lead?
   - What are (geo)political and cultural trends that can have a business impact?

> P&G Morocco was going to be hit by a major disruption: the government's decision to open borders. So far, the production facilities could be highly unproductive because tariffs kept competition out. That was going to change. Unless we acted fast, and fixed the business, in a couple of years we'd be wiped off the marketplace by new entrants and increased rivalry. In an open economy, the plants could only be kept going if they were completely overhauled.

True, P&G could in the future also source from other, better performing production sites outside Morocco. That's absolutely valid. However, we are also talking about the livelihoods of a lot of local families. We saw it as our duty to at least try to keep as many jobs safe as possible. A leader must care enough to give it his or her best in this respect.

2. **Understand the profit model.**
   - Where is the profit today? Where will it be in the future?
   - Where does our company make money? Often, only five to seven markets or brands make most of the money.
   - How do we make money? What is our place in the value chain? Are there profit pools out there we should tap into?
   - Are there profit swamps? Areas that just suck up money and resources that might never yield a return?

The key question was: why could P&G Poland sell Pampers and Always 50% cheaper and yet make a double-digit margin when we were losing money? How could other emerging markets thrive with the same brand mix? The reason for the lack of profitability was that Morocco was trapped in a negative spiral. We called it the Moroccan Paradox (see figure 3).

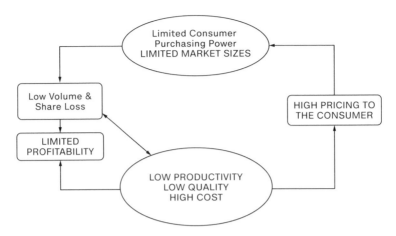

Figure 3: The Moroccan Paradox (© 2023 Peter Corijn / VUCASTAR)

Because of low productivity, the cost of doing business was very high. This led to high pricing. But consumers had only limited purchasing power. This in turn limited market sizes. With the significant volume losses due to quality and marketing issues, volume went down further. That meant less scale and capacity used in the plants, which made cost rise. But high cost required high pricing… You get the problem.

It was important to take this helicopter view and to focus on what was 'destiny changing'. For instance, Hair Care needed better advertising. But it would not be destiny changing. Getting out of this negative spiral was.

3. **Assess the organization.**
   - Do we have the right talent to succeed?
   - Is the leadership strong enough?
   - Do we have a growth culture? A culture that is agile and resilient enough to tackle the challenges ahead?

Numerous functions showed subpar performance. It was unlikely that every employee had suddenly become incompetent or intentionally came to work to do a poor job. We were confident that we had hired highly capable individuals. It was evident that there was a systemic leadership and culture issue that needed to be addressed.

4. **Review the Competition.**
   - Do a SWOT analysis (Strengths/Weakness/Opportunities/Threats).

Unilever's Omo detergent brand was the key competitor to challenge. They had the momentum and no obvious weakness. P&G had to catch up first in just about all areas of the Laundry detergent marketing mix and then try to recreate a competitive advantage.

   - How would you think and act if you were a competitor?
   - How and where do competitors make their money?

Let's now do an exercise on those two questions. First, consider yourself in charge of an anti-drug agency and tasked with devising countermeasures against drug cartels. Next, imagine yourself as the CEO of a large cocaine empire. That industry is estimated to be worth $90bn worldwide according to UN statistics. The biggest market is the USA ($36bn).

Consumption over there had declined somewhat of late but that had been largely offset by gains in the EU ($34bn). Global growth is estimated at >30% per annum.

One day, as you are gently polishing your cherished fleet of limited-edition Ferraris and Lamborghinis, an executive team member brings the news that 2,000 hectares of cocaine plantations have just been destroyed. Do you care? It's unfortunate but it does not matter. Let's look at the value chain.[1]

ITEM	Price - USD
350 kilograms of dried coca leaves:	385
1 kilogram of dried coca leaves:	1.1
Converted into one kilo of cocaine. Price in Columbia:	800
Ready for export:	2,200
Imported into the USA:	14,500
Transfer to mid-level dealers:	19,500
Price at street-level dealers:	78,000
'Real' price after the pure kilo has been cut:	122,000

These margins make it the single most profitable criminal activity in the history of mankind. The leader of the Medellìn cartel, Pablo Escobar, made the Forbes list of the ten richest people in the world (nr. 7). Nobody knew how much he was worth. His accountant, brother Roberto Escobar, estimates that $2,500 had to be spent each month on rubber bands, just to hold the money together. They could even afford to lose 10% of their cash every year. It was eaten by rats, destroyed by water damage, or simply misplaced somewhere in their hundreds of stash places.[2]

As the value chain clearly shows, even if the cost of the coca leaves were to double - because the supply is now more limited - it would only make a small percentage of difference in your profit model. On top, there are masses of suppliers (farmers) in your growing region but only one buyer for their produce: you. New buyers cannot come in because it is an illegal activity, and you have the muscle to keep them out. That means that any cost increase can be shoved on to the shoulders of farmers. Anyway, there has been so much innovation in production methods that extraction yields have dramatically increased.

However, the next day brings more worrying news. Your associates have lost control of Ciudad Juàrez, a border town right up the US border. Now that's a different matter altogether. Control of one of the few good entry points into the world's largest market is essential. The price of a kilo goes up seven times by the simple fact of moving it one meter across the border. Your competitors know this too. You must get it back, whatever the cost. That's why the violence in those entry towns is often completely out of control.

You're about to light a Cohiba Behike (at $450 a pop) to recover from that last report, when information comes in that a police action in one of your key towns in the US has made the cost of doing business harder. Your area manager sends a recommendation to increase price by 10% to sustain profits. Do you approve it? Yes, you do, because the market is inelastic, meaning that a price increase leads to very little volume loss. It's an addictive product after all. Admittedly, your consumer research data are patchy, but experience indicates that a 10% price increase leads to maximum 1% less consumption. Let's say, a gram in the streets is sold at $100. A kilo is sold each week for $100,000. Due to better policing and the consequent 10% price increase, only 990 grams is sold per week. Revenue is $108,900. You were wise to go ahead with the price increase. These are the sort of insights needed to define effective competitive strategy for your business.

5. Ensure that you obtain input from employees on the frontline.

It can be as straightforward as setting up a weekly pizza lunch with a couple of colleagues, with open enrollment for anyone from any department or level within the company. Set three conditions: (i) they must speak their mind candidly, (ii) everything they say is off the record, (iii) everything you say is on the record.

6. It might be useful to involve an external consultant.

Before the strategy meeting, the consultant can conduct a 30-minute interview with each executive and subsequently act as a facilitator during the strategy review. This is because human nature can sometimes make people less forthcoming with their genuine opinions in the presence of the CEO. The consultant can provide the alternative viewpoints without any executive being at risk.

Let's now review some essential concepts to keep in mind as one develops strategy before an in-depth review of the strategic choices at P&G Morocco in chapter 4.

EXECUTIVE SUMMARY:

1. There is essential prework required before the strategy discussion.
2. The most critical part is to fully understand the profit model.
3. Assess your organization.
4. Review the competition.
5. Get the input from employees on the frontline.
6. Consider involving an external consultant.

CHAPTER 3

The Issue with Killing an Opponent and Nine More Considerations When Developing Strategy

In this section, we will explore ten vital factors to consider while undertaking a strategic exercise. A series of stories will be told to illustrate the point. Some are not related to business. They are nevertheless highly relevant. Each time a key insight is drawn from them.

1. **Make hard choices, relevant to the industry. Be specific. Avoid 'straddling'.**

In Michael E. Porter's seminal HBR article[1] and further writings inspired by him, strategy is defined as:

- 'An integrated set of choices, leading to different activities from rivals, that position a firm in an industry so as to create sustainable advantage and deliver superior financial results relative to competition.'[2]

All words matter but none more than 'choice'. It's also the most difficult part. Everybody supports it, until it is done to their detriment. Cut 20% of an executive's budget and take his top managers away – because of different choices – and watch what happens. Yet, hard calls on what to do and what not to do are the very essence of good strategy.

Avoid truisms and cliches. Take the following test: stand in front of your organization and tell them: 'We want to win.' All will applaud. I do not think anybody will raise a finger to say: 'Erm, not me actually. I so enjoy being a total loser.' These sorts of statements have little strategic value. Nobody will argue the opposite. That's a good test: ***if the opposite is not an option, then the strategy is probably not choiceful enough***. Allow me to clarify that point further via a journey into rock & roll.

Most rock bands only have a short shelf life. Audiences are fickle. Youth culture constantly changes, and with it, fashion, and music tastes. Every new generation looks down on the clothes and music of the previous one. Genres can lose relevance fast, almost overnight. In a band, one is constantly living with the other guys. After several years, they just tire of each other's company. As the saying goes: 'How can I miss you if you never leave?' Even brothers get into regular fisticuffs. Those who followed the antics of the Gallaghers in Britpop band Oasis are well aware of it. The Davies' brothers from The Kinks have a difficult relationship lasting to this day. When I saw then 71-year-old Ray Davies on stage in 2015, he still could not resist a jibe at his brother Dave. He said: 'In The Kinks, Dave was The and I was Kinks' (quite funny that actually).

Believe it or not, it can be a hard life. Metal band Mötley Crüe had a number 1 album in *Dr. Feelgood* at the end of 1989. After two years of non-stop touring to promote this record, they went on strike to obtain a two-week break (admittedly, their lifestyle would even have exhausted Hercules in mid-season form).[3] A top guitar player like Steve Lukather (a.o. Toto) has to spend 200 days on the road each year.[4]

Despite all that, U2 has been around for 40 years. I sometimes ask students to develop the strategy for the Irish band. One choice that comes out 100% of the time is the following: 'We will be a good team'. That is true but also useless as a strategy. The reason is that no band starts out with a desire to be a bad team. Nobody marries to get divorced. In other words, the opposite of the strategy is not an option. The question is: 'What makes for a good team in the music industry?' (Or for that matter, what makes for a good team in your industry?)

Let's do an analysis of what happens in a rock band, investigating a vital part from the strategy pre-work list (chapter 2): how does the profit model work?

The songwriter makes most of the money in the form of royalties. Few drummers write songs. After (fictional) band The Sea of Poppies had a first hit album, royalties started to pour in. The band's songwriter, Suneet, now arrives in a fancy sportscar to rehearsals. Neil, the drummer, took the bus. He's thinking: 'Wait a minute, I'm part of this band, my drum sound is unique, it defines the band. Why am I not making as much?' It starts to eat the fellow. Neil's girlfriend wholeheartedly agrees with him. Resentment grows.

The band has another songwriter, Andrew. Frankly, his songs are mediocre. Suneet told him so. Andrew's ego is bruised. He also knows that getting songs on the next album means that he will make a lot more money. So, he fights to get his average compositions included. Suneet now has the choice to accept that and settle for a less good album, or risk breaking up the band.

All band members make money when they play concerts. Jasmin, the bass player, is pushing for more touring. Suneet doesn't feel like it. His wife is pregnant, and he wants to spend more time at home. Anyway, he can afford to because royalties are coming in. Suneet often wonders why he stays with that band anyway. After all, he writes the hits, he's the genius of the band. Look at Bruce Springsteen, Sting or David Bowie, they managed well enough on their own, didn't they?

So, for a rock band, a good team strategy needs to resolve the inevitable tension created by the money question. U2 decided right from the start to go for the 'All for One, One for All' strategy. They divide all income by five: 20% for each band member and a fifth for manager Paul McGuinness. That way, all felt equally rewarded. It focused efforts on making the best U2 album, not on one person's song. They always portray all band members equally on album sleeves (ego management does matter too). Even John Lydon – a.k.a. Johnny Rotten from the infamous Sex Pistols – came to understand this: 'You got to stop the nonsense of 'I wrote this' and 'I wrote that' – share the money and stay well with each other.'[5] Bands are often born out of a group of friends, passionate about music. Over time, it becomes a business, a living to pay the mortgage. It's show *business* after all. The U2 case illustrates that strategy needs to be specific and relevant to a given industry.

Another watch-out is to avoid 'straddling'. Once a strategic choice is made, one must live up to it. A budget airline positioned on the lowest fares cannot offer excellent cabin service and food on a par with Singapore Airlines. A premium airline may find it hard to also run a budget airline. British Airways tried that with *Go Fly* (styled as *Go*) in 1998. It did not work. In May 2002, Go was bought by rival budget airline EasyJet and later merged into EasyJet's operations. You cannot be everything to everybody. To quote a wonderful Porsche tagline: 'It's not about being something to everyone, but everything to someone' (a nice line for your next Valentine's card by the way).

2. Always thoroughly think through unintended consequences.

'What shall we do about Sheikh Yassin?'[6] It became increasingly clear to Israeli leaders that the founder and spiritual leader of the terrorist organization Hamas would need to be neutralized.* Events that took place on January 2004 decided the issue. A 21-year-old female from the Gaza strip detonated a bomb at the Erez border crossing into Israel. Four people were killed and ten more injured. The next day, Sheikh Yassin called a press conference. He was overjoyed that for the first time a woman had been used instead of a male. That was a change from the past. Before, the Sheikh had issued fatwas against the use of female suicide bombers. Now, he saw it as a most welcome development.

Israel was rather less thrilled with these new tactics. It is harder to examine Arab women than men. 'Even in a dirty war, there are standards of decorum', said Defence Minister Mofaz. It increased the risk of attacks and explosives being smuggled in. Importantly, there was a secret recording available that had the Sheikh directly ordering his operational staff to use women as suicide bombers. This ensured internal legal support to go after Yassin. On March 22, 2004, two

---

* Hamas is designated as a terrorist organization by Israel, the E.U., the USA, Canada and Japan.

successively launched missiles made Sheikh Yassin and several of his bodyguards shahids (martyrs). Eventually Hamas sued for a truce.

Mission success. Or so one would think. There was one major flaw in the plan that lead to the unintended consequence of strengthening Hamas. Sheikh Yassin had been totally opposed to working with Iran (because of the Sunni/Shia schism). He imposed this view on the entire organization. But his successors had no such qualms. Hamas succeeded in gaining total control of Gaza, kicking out competitor Fatah (the PLO's party) in a brief civil war, thanks to massive assistance from Teheran. Had Sheikh Yassin been kept alive, this might have been impossible.

It's important to allocate time for contemplating whether the decisions made could result in significantly different or unforeseen outcomes than those initially intended.

3. Make sure that your strategy captures barriers to entry. At least, think about it.

Profit is a miracle considering that everybody wants to take it from you. Suppliers want better prices, buyers insist on higher margins, unions claim a better pension deal, employees demand a salary increase and the government sure would like a bigger slice of the cake. High margins attract new entrants. Competition wants your money too.

There's no way to keep rivals out. It's also illegal for good reasons because free markets benefit consumers and innovation. However, nothing prevents you to legally make it as hard as possible for others to snatch your daily bread. Or to take your best friend away: diamonds. De Beers is a $5bn company specialized in diamond exploitation and trading. Today, they control about 35% of rough diamond distribution. Via their sightholder and auction sales business, the firm still manages to keep prices high. The company romanced the stone via their selling line: 'A Diamond is Forever'. Alas, happy days seemed over. A serious substitute threat to the model materialized in the shape of man-made diamonds.

A natural diamond is made from carbon over a period of one to three billion years under very specific conditions. Carbon is put under very high pressure at least 140 km under the earth's crust at high temperature. Eventually, via molten rock, it finds its way closer to the surface. In a man-made diamond those billion years can be reduced to weeks with the same properties as a natural one. Except that it is cheaper. Industrial usage and retail volume of these kept growing. *Blood Diamond* also had an impact. It's a gem of a film, but it showed the ugly side of African diamond exploitation and its horrific human toll. Millennials especially started to feel uncomfortable with natural diamonds and went for the more affordable alternative. How to defend? De Beers initially took legal action and obtained the ruling that man-made diamonds must be called 'synthetic diamonds'. That cheapened the image considerably, thus creating a barrier to entry. Few men would say: 'Baby I love you so much that I bought you synthetic diamonds' (prepare for a night on the sofa).

De Beers then took the difficult decision to get into synthetic diamond production as well. Their strategy is to make prices as low as possible in that category. 1 carat (i.e. 0.2 grams) of a 'real' diamond is on average $6,000. Man-made is now offered as low as $800. The low pricing is designed to do two things: (i) widen the gap between the two types of stones, (ii) keep margins low in synthetic to discourage other investors to enter the category. A downside might be that by this move, they are further legitimizing synthetic diamonds.

> **The P&G Morocco Challenge – barriers to entry:**
>
> As mentioned in the pre-work, when Morocco opened its borders for free trade as of 2001, more competitors would inevitably enter. They would first go into the so-called 'modern trade', national chains. Getting listed is often only a question of money and an attractive margin offer. But to get into thousands of small shops and especially rural shops is a different matter. It is complex and very expensive. It only makes sense if you have the scale to offset the cost. Hence, this could be an area where we could benefit from an existing barrier to entry.
>
> The first job was to know where the rural villages were. Many were not on any maps. Our Sales Force sent out people with GPSs touring even the remotest areas. Every time they found a hamlet, they would type in the coordinates. By the end of the exercise, nobody except for the Army had that information. Next, a sophisticated distribution network was set up, a whole pyramid of wholesalers ending in small stores in villages. These shops were tiny but often allowed those running them to double their income. If you only make $2 per day, and can now earn $4 per day, that makes a significant difference.

We also had to do better marketing there. One of the reasons why less was known about these places was simply that it is not always pleasant to go to rural markets. Farmers get up at first daylight. Going on a storecheck can mean hitting the road at 4a.m., driving long hours, and spending time in a dusty place where you are not entirely sure you should trust the drinks and food on offer. On top, many recruits in the company were from urban higher social classes (they had the funds to study, often abroad at French universities). Rural was not well known by them. We had to – using the words of then CEO A.G. Lafley – get 'in touch'. Some marketeers went to live with a rural family for a couple of days. We broadened our knowledge base considerably. Rural moved from a lost area into a powerhouse for P&G.

4. Understand and create your profit zone. Make sure to have strategic control points.

Sometimes a business book creates enlightenment. For me, it was Messrs. Slywotzky & Morrison's *The Profit Zone*.[7] If you read one more business book, make it this one. It outlines how to structure your enterprise to achieve lasting profitability. Highly profitable companies achieve their results because of clear decisions on four vectors:

a. <u>Customer Selection</u>: who do we want to serve, and not serve? When I worked on Gillette, we did a yearly PPUPY analysis, profit per user per year. If there was no profit in a certain audience, we'd not engage in it.

b. <u>Value Capture</u>: how do I get rewarded for the value I create? There is a big difference between creating value and getting paid for it.

c. <u>Create strategic control points</u>: As previously stated, generating profits is no mean feat. It is important to strive for at least one, and preferably two, control points to safeguard your profits. Below is a summary of various strategic control points and their effectiveness in protecting profits.

STRATEGIC CONTROL POINT	STRENGTH
Commodity with cost disadvantage	none
Commodity with cost parity	none
Commodity with 10 to 20% cost advantage	low
One-year product lead	low
Two-year development lead	medium
Brand, copyright	medium
Own the customer relationship	high
Lovemark	high
Superdominant share position	high
Manage the value chain	high
Own the standard	high
Patent	high
Network effects	high
Monopoly	super high but illegal

Why is owning the standard a great control point? The reason is that the cost to change is major. Once a whole organization runs on Microsoft, it can be expensive to move to something else. Imagine you had to change the standard width of the whole network of railway tracks. The cost would be prohibitive. It would also require a change of all the rolling stock.

Brands are a strategic control point because they enhance loyalty and trust. Loyal customers are the most profitable because they create return business without the need of constant seduction by costly promotions. Brands also mitigate risk. If you travel in a very exotic place where your stomach and digestive system are not ready to survive the local fare, McDonalds is a great choice. You know their standards are the same everywhere. You can trust that burger, but perhaps not the local street food stall. IMD Professor Gautham Challagalla's formula for Brand Value captures that dimension well: Brand Value = Benefit – Cost – Risk. Consumers are especially willing to pay more if the brand conveys status. Some brands convey identity signals. They tell us and others who we are. We are willing to pay for that privilege.

d. <u>Reflect it in a Go-to-Market Model</u>: These are so important that the entire chapter 5 is spent on this topic.

5. Examine the key drivers of profit in an industry before entering it.

When considering an acquisition or merger outside of your core business, make an in-depth understanding of the industry profit model part of the due diligence process. If not, you'll join the statistic that at least 70% of acquisitions fail. Industries and companies do operate on very specific profit models. You might be seduced by some of their margins to enter the fray but without that knowledge, an unpleasant surprise might await. Let's discuss one of them.

The pharmaceutical industry operates on a 'blockbuster model'. This means that a couple of hugely successful products pay most of the bills. These are protected by the strategic control point of patents. Just to give one example, anti-depressant Prozac was 30% of Eli Lilly's turnover. However, to get one hit, a massive number of molecules must be developed and tested. Most fail to make the long and rigorous qualification process. It's expensive in terms of R&D. On average, it is estimated that it takes about ten years for a new medicine to complete the journey from initial discovery to the marketplace. Clinical trials alone take six to seven years on average. The average cost to research and develop each successful drug often exceeds $1bn. Consequently, unless one has that R&D capability and the funds to fuel the effort, an entry into big pharma is not a good idea.

6. **Challenge yourself to set the strategic scene, to move the battlefield to your advantage, to control the options.**

Sometimes one finds oneself between a rock and a hard place. Such was the situation of Rudolf Virchow. He was a celebrated German scientist and liberal politician (1821–1907), considered 'the father of modern pathology'. The German Iron Chancellor, Otto von Bismarck, became so angry with the constant criticisms thrown at him by Mr. Virchow that he challenged the latter to a duel.

That was a somewhat unpleasant situation. If the scientist killed the Chancellor, the favorite of the emperor and the second most powerful man in the German Reich, it would not go down well. But the alternative, to lose and die, was not particularly appealing either. If the usual pistols or swords were used, the latter was the most likely outcome.

Mr. Virchow decided to seize control back. He let the Chancellor know that as the challenged party, he was entitled to choose the weapons. He presented two identical sausages to von Bismarck. He said: 'One of these is infected with deadly germs, the other perfectly sound. Let His Excellency decide which one he wishes to eat, and I will eat the other.'

A message was promptly sent that the Chancellor had decided to cancel the duel.[8]

> **The P&G Morocco Challenge – strategic control:**
>
> Running ahead of the next chapter on P&G Morocco's strategy, it was decided that the restructuring was a must-do. It was unpleasant but the only way to keep the company going was to increase productivity. Cost does walk on legs as well.
>
> The challenge was that P&G had signed an investment agreement related to Pampers. One paragraph promised a specific number of extra jobs. In return, the government had agreed to reduce import duties on raw materials. The positive PR around the agreement had been considerable, involving even His Majesty the King. At the time, this was an excellent initiative. Alas, with the total collapse of Tide, the situation had significantly changed. As the new GM, I'd have to announce: 'Salam aleikum folks, I know we signed this recently, but we actually need to fire at least 200 employees.'

Legal advice was not clear. It was a fix like the one Mr. Virchow found himself in. If we were asked: 'Did you know this at the time of signing the agreement?' a 'yes' answer would qualify us as liars, a 'no' answer as incompetent. What was certain was that we had to go and see all senior members of the government before any action was taken.

The team found the right angle by looking at the issue more broadly. Our restructuring was also a much-needed response to the government's own policy of open borders. We fully supported this as we were in favour of free trade but had no other choice than to prepare as soon as possible. If we were not competitive, P&G would sooner or later decide to source from better-placed plants, all of which would spell trouble for the local production facilities. This was perfectly true.

The other fact we highlighted was that P&G would offer less jobs but the country's employment would not suffer. One third of those leaving received an attractive early retirement package. Another third would be replaced with better-qualified, younger people. Youth unemployment was a major headache for the government. The last third was simply outsourced. P&G did not need to do its own security or garden maintenance. It could be done cheaper by outside suppliers. The government did understand our plight. After lots more adventures, some of which I'll talk about later, the restructuring was a success.

As demonstrated by these stories, there is always a means to regain strategic control, although it may require innovative thinking to identify it.

7. Make sure to prioritize the core business unless there is a strategic inflection point. If you can, lead the shift. In case a competitor does it, formulate a counter-strategy.

How much in a strategy should be about the existing business and how much about the new? The Dutch proverb rightly states: 'To possess is to possess, but to acquire is an art.'* Protecting the core business, and building it, is the minimum a strategy should achieve. At the same time, it is important to look ahead. Google's ex-CEO Eric Schmidt came up with the 70/20/10 model. It's interesting that even a high-tech company focuses most of its efforts on the core:
- 70% of the organization's capacity is dedicated to the core business;
- 20% to projects related to the core business;
- 10% of their capacity is spent on unrelated new businesses.[9]

A study in a Harvard Business Review article reported that companies using a similar model outperformed their peers via a price-to-earnings premium of 10 to 20%.[10] This is therefore an interesting model to follow.

The above is no longer valid when a market incurs a 'strategic inflection point'. Intel's Andrew S. Grove defined it as 'the time in the life of a business when its fundamentals are about to change… when something is changing in a big way …when the balance of forces shifts from the old structure, from the old ways of doing business and the old ways of competing, to the new.'[11] Then the core is being made irrelevant.

---

* 'Hebben is hebben en krijgen is kunst'

I call it *a game changer: a strategic initiative, product, idea or process that completely changes the name of the game*. It is best to lead it. But sometimes it is done unto us. It sure is easy to miss it, as happened in the music industry. That industry lived a bonanza time in the 80s. Consumers still bought newly released records. Not only that, CDs were also bought to replace the vinyl albums music fans already had in their collection. The market had firmly moved to albums, on which the profit was higher than on singles. With the onset of the digital revolution, the emergence of Napster in 1999 was a game changer. It allowed for the free exchange of digitized MP3 song files, presenting a significant challenge to the traditional music business. In response, the industry, Metallica, and Dr. Dre filed lawsuits against the platform for enabling thievery and copyright infringement. Although these efforts proved successful in bankrupting Napster in June 2022, the digital genie was out of the bottle.

Music labels should have recognized the game-changing shift and created their own digital offering. Sony had brought us the Walkman but missed the new digital player market. Apple seized the opportunity with the launch of the iPod and iTunes in October 2001. It was a breakthrough. One could now hold thousands of songs in a superbly designed pocket device. The additional benefit was that via iTunes, music fans could download just the one hit song from a certain band. People were fed up with having to buy a full album for the one or two songs they wanted. A single song on iTunes was priced at 99 cents and music labels received 55% of the sale. However, they could also have asked a percentage of each iPod sold, as the device would be useless without the song library. The primary goal of Apple's creation of iTunes was to drive sales of iPods, which proved to be a wildly successful product with 450 million units sold. Unfortunately for the music labels, they missed out on a significant opportunity to generate additional revenue. Even a 1% royalty on each iPod sold could have resulted in an extra $1bn.

Jimmy Iovine, co-founder of Interscope Records, responded differently to the digital threat. As soon as he saw Napster, he realized that the game was up. He did spot that quality cool headphones would become an important business in the MP3 player world. With superstar rapper and producer Dr. Dre, he started 'Beats Electronics'. The brand was sold for a whopping $3bn to Apple in 2014.

The emergence of streaming platforms (Spotify, Deezer, Apple Music) has once again completely transformed the music industry. Nowadays, it's rare for individuals to even own a CD player and the iTunes app has been discontinued. Vinyl is making a modest come-back. But the disruption is far from over.

The latest challenge to labels is the arrival of AI-generated music. Platforms such as Boomy allow you to compose a song in a matter of minutes. Since 2019, it's estimated that Boomy's AI has already produced 12 million songs. Endel provides users with personalized soundscapes to aid relaxation, focus, and sleep, with 35 million tracks created to-date. However, there are concerns about copyright infringement, particularly in relation to Google's MusicLM technology, which was trained using 280,000 hours of existing music and songs. While some argue that AI-generated music is derivative work, others disagree. It seems likely that courts will be busy settling disputes in the years to come. Regardless, it's clear that AI will continue to advance, and there will be no stopping its impact.

A revolution in digital artistry may be imminent. FN Meka*, a digital artist with over ten million followers on TikTok, has already been signed by Capitol Records. Artist Praga Khan from Lords of Acid is at the forefront of this groundbreaking trend. According to him, the virtual artist market is presently valued at $4.6 billion and growing at a 20% rate. Moreover, there's a significant opportunity for virtual artists to endorse brands. As Praga humorously quipped: 'They never get old, don't drink and drive, and don't engage in rock & roll excess.'[12] Certainly, music bands and their management will need to familiarize themselves with Web3, NFTs, the Metaverse, Fan Tokens,** their digital twins, and how blockchain will manage their royalties and rights in the future.

Shifting our focus to another industry, Philip Morris International ('PMI' – the world's largest tobacco company) decided to create the strategic inflection point themselves. Their industry is not one that needs tarot cards to foretell the future.

Do this quiz, answering yes or no:
- Will there be more tobacco regulation?
- Will there be more restrictions on smoking?
- Will cigarette volumes continue to decline?

---

* FN Meka was dropped by the label after two weeks over racist stereotyping.

** Web3: a decentralized ecosystem based on blockchain; NFT: Non-Fungible Token; the Metaverse: a 3D-enabled space that allows you to have lifelike personal and business experiences online; Fan Tokens: a type of cryptocurrency or digital asset, they grant fans access rights, privileges and other perks.

- Will excise taxes go up?
- Is smoking bad for you?

Yes, on all counts. In the face of these dynamics, PMI decided to fully commit to a smoke-free future by offering a portfolio of reduced risk products. An estimated 60% of marketing spend goes to these. That's quite a gutsy move since they have the most successful (and highly profitable) cigarette brand in Marlboro.

It took PMI ten years and an estimated $6bn to develop brands like IQOS. It's a heat not burn ('HNB') product. A short 'Heet' stick is inserted in an electronic IQOS device. Exactly as the name indicates, tobacco is heated instead of burned, which reduces toxic elements. The U.S. Food and Drug Administration authorized the marketing of IQOS (via Altria) as a modified risk product. It's a multi-billion $ business today. In core market Japan, they own >50% of the HNB segment (30% of the total market). The expansion goes ahead worldwide. The real breakthrough could come if – as the CEO hinted – governments could be persuaded that there is now a viable alternative to getting rid of cigarettes altogether. That would move the market in PMI's favor.

Looking back, it may seem straightforward, but it's a different story when you're in the thick of it or attempting to persuade others internally to adopt a game-changing idea. It's very hard to walk away from a proven and profitable model. James Michael Lafferty, CEO of Fine Hygienic Holding, believes that controversy is an inevitable part of proposing a breakthrough concept: 'if 99% of your team agree with an idea, it is not breakthrough.'

Things can become very challenging when a game changer successfully enters your market space. At that point, you may consider seven strategic options to defend:

a) Retreat: give up, cut your losses.
b) Buy the game changer. The acquisition can be used to neutralize the threat, or to develop a new business model. For instance, tobacco giant Imperial Brands ('IBG') bought the e-vapor technology and patent from inventor Hon Lik in 2013. It lead to the foundation of IBG's Fontem start-up, active in developing potentially lower risk smoking products.
c) Strengthen and transform the core business to fend off incoming rivals.
d) Be a fast follower, particularly when there is an opportunity to improve and innovate upon the offering of the successful pioneer.
e) Milk the core business. Alas this won't last. But it can be a way to fund the sixth option until that new promising business is up and running.
f) Develop new game-changing business models yourself and disrupt somebody else's business; as Beats Electronics did.
g) Go and cry to mommy and daddy and ask for help. Said differently, lobby the government for restrictive regulation and lots of subsidies. Add tears and 'we are too big to fail. If we fail it will be much, much worse for you' (this is a theoretical example of course).[13]

8. **Hope is not a strategy. It's important to develop clear building blocks on how the strategic goals can be achieved.**

In the movie *Dumb and Dumber* (a guilty pleasure), one of the dumb guys, Lloyd Christmas (Jim Carrey), falls in love with attractive Mary Swanson (Lauren Holly). At some point, he confronts her and asks what his chances are. Mary states that they are not good. Lloyd asks if she means not good like one out of a hundred. Mary replies that it's more like one out of a million. The guy is dazed for a moment but then lights up with a smile: 'So you're telling me there is a chance! YEAAHHH!' It's never going to happen, not with these odds. The same applies to your strategic choices. They should not solely be based on hope and optimism. If a major profit gap is left in the forecast, without viable ideas on how to fill it, that profit hole tends to still be there at the end of the year.

9. **Leave your ego at the door in strategy reviews.**

A little-known fact about WWI is that in 1917, the German peace party gained an ascendancy over the Kaiser. They offered France to end the war, to withdraw and give the region of Alsace-Lorraine back to France (Germany had annexed it after the 1871 war). The proposal was killed by the inflated ego of one man, Alexandre-Felix-Joseph Ribot. Mr. Ribot was the French minister for Foreign Affairs. He deeply resented the fact that the peace offer had been made to Prime Minister Aristide Briant, instead of through him and the Foreign Office. Ribot torpedoed the peace proposal. The British allies were kept completely in the dark. The rejection of the offer moved the Kaiser back towards the war-party. Mr.

Ribot was ultimately fired when these facts became known. But I'm not sure that is sufficient consolation for the hundreds of thousands killed or maimed for life in another year of mindless slaughter.[14] On top, the Peace Treaty of Versailles incapsulated the seeds for the next world war.

If there are any instances of egotistical behaviour within your organization, it's preferable to insist on transparency and a degree of humility during the strategy review.

10. Digital is an enabler to create and capture customer value. Digital by itself is a tool.

'Digital' will come up in strategy reviews. It should. However, digital by itself is not a strategy. Why do we watch Netflix? Because it is digital? No, digital is the enabler. We like it because Netflix delivers customer empowerment. The technology allows us to choose what we want to watch, when, without these annoying advertising breaks. They also capitalized on a great insight: we love binge watching. On TV, a new episode is broadcast every week. But Netflix releases all episodes of a season in one go. Apple did not put record labels out of business. Not having to purchase entire albums and the convenience of carrying a thousand songs on a pocket-sized iPod device were the contributing factors.

A digital transformation only has merit in as far as it creates value. Not unlike in a 'regular' business, one either delivers better cost, a better experience or a platform that has value as per the Digital Vortex in figure 4.[15]

COST VALUE	EXPERIENCE VALUE	PLATFORM VALUE
• Free / Ultra Low Cost • Buyer Aggregation • Price Transparency • Reverse Auctions • Consumption-Based Pricing	• Customer Empowerment • Customization • Instant Gratification • Reduced Friction • Automation	• Ecosystem • Crowdsourcing • Communities • Digital Marketplace • Data Orchestrator

Figure 4: The Digital Vortex (Source: Global Center for Digital Business Transformation, 2015
From: J. Loucks, J. Macaulay, A. Noronha, M. Wade, 'Digital Vortex')

Once again, one must understand the profit model of both the company and industry when making bold digital decisions. Not knowing anything about the business, when confronted with a case study on what a newspaper should do in the digital age, my initial reaction was to make a digital newspaper and to ensure that the content was even more attractive to readers. Frankly, that approach would have led to bankruptcy. It was entirely the wrong problem to solve. One would walk in what Harvard Business School Professor Bharat Anand calls 'The Content Trap'.[16]

Let's start with understanding the traditional newspaper model. In most cities, there are only a couple of newspapers. Fixed costs are high: journalists on the payroll, printing presses, distribution costs. Without sufficient scale, one cannot make it work. Newspaper subscription was only a small part of the profit model. The sale of advertising space was more important. Here newspapers had some negotiation power. There was only so much ad space available and there are only a couple of newspapers with attractive circulation. But most profitable of all were the classifieds.

Classifieds margins are great for two reasons. Firstly, the people placing them are many and hence do not have bargaining power. The key driver however is a network effect coming from platform value (see the Vortex on the previous page). People only have interest in placing their small ad if there are sufficient readers. Readers are interested in scanning classifieds only if there are lots of listings. Imagine you are looking for a car. One newspaper has two cars listed on average, another 200. Which newspaper do you turn to? That creates a positive feedback loop as more readers are of course of interest to those selling their car. It is the classifieds which create a 'winner take all' effect and explain the limited number of newspapers in each city.[17] Classifieds were the subsidy for the news. When the Internet showed up, the threat to the newspaper's profit model was not on 'news'. That impact was small. But it was massive for classifieds. Consumers moved to specialized online sites for holiday homes, jobs and real estate. That effectively killed the cash cow.

Axel Springer is one of Europe's largest media houses. They a.o. publish Die Welt and Bild. That company had a successful digital transformation. They did create subscriber-based online news, but much more critically, acquired a roster of profitable start-ups playing in the advertising and classifieds space. In other words, digital allowed them to continue to capture value.[18]

CHAPTER 4

'From Darkness to Light' – Tools Used, Strategic Choices, and Outcome at P&G Morocco

It must be supreme irony by the gods that the Monitor Consulting company founded by Mr. Porter – the pre-eminent authority on strategy – went bankrupt. Since 2011, Monitor is part of Deloitte. However, many of their tools remain totally valid. Certainly, none more than 'Choice Cascading'. It's brilliant in its simplicity. We used it to define a new strategy for P&G Morocco.

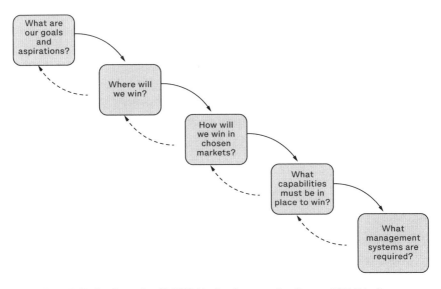

Figure 6: Choice Cascading (© 2000 Monitor Company, Inc. Source: P&G / Monitor Strategy Seminar 2001)

Everything starts with: 'What do you want?' Having a goal of obtaining a basic level of fitness is markedly distinct from striving to win an Olympic medal. This disparity leads to distinct strategic choices. In order to attain a basic level of fitness, dedicating 30 minutes daily to exercise is typically adequate. One can maintain a regular job and simply train in the morning or evening without the need for additional support. However, achieving the level of an Olympic champion necessitates complete dedication. It requires a lifestyle commitment, day and night. A support team comprising a coach, nutritionist, sponsors, and more, must be assembled.

To achieve your goals, you must determine where you can win. This involves choosing geographies, product lines, consumer and trade segments, and considering your position in the value chain. Once those decisions have been made, ***the next step is to define how to win in the chosen areas. This, in turn, necessitates the development of appropriate capabilities and competencies, as well as management systems.***

It's also important to work backward. Executional concerns are already part of the equation. Available capabilities can define strategic choice. The means must match the objective. For instance, the chances of winning an Olympic swimming medal are slim for a 1.70 meter tall male. He might train hard, but has a genetic disadvantage versus athletes who measure two meters and train just as hard. The same applies to basketball. Our not-so-tall male might do well to choose soccer in the 'where-to-play' choice. At least if the aspiration is to make it to the top. Diego Maradona: 1.65 meters, Lionel Messi 1.70, Neymar da Silva Santos Júnior 1.75. Or Formula 1 racing: Lewis Hamilton: 1.70, Alain Prost 1.65,

Ayrton Senna 1.75, Jackie Stewart 1.63. Racing of course has other challenges. There are only 20 drivers in F1, and it is very expensive to get there.

Just to say: play to your strengths and be aware of your limitations. Be brutally honest about it. Sometimes to give all you got is not enough through no fault of your own. Like not having the lithe flexible body of a prima ballerina though your dream was to be a dancer in the Bolshoi. It's no different in business. What is, is. What isn't, isn't. *Feel free to state what you will not do.* That too drives focus of the organization.

The strategic discussion outcome was captured in a one-page document, the 'OGSM' (short for 'Objective, Goals, Strategies, Measures').

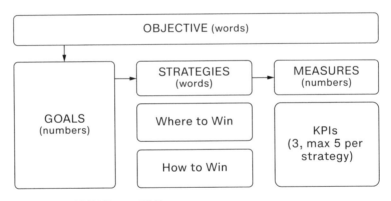

Figure 7: The OGSM (Source: P&G)

This is how the tool operates: begin with stating the Objective, which is the central aspiration. The Goals should be quantifiable, and it's recommended to limit them to five to seven at most, as having too many goals can cause a loss of focus. Next, express the Strategies in words. The final component to develop is the Measures section, as what gets measured gets accomplished. Be cautious not to include too many Key Performance Indicators (KPIs), only those that make a substantial difference. It must be a one-page document (in legible font size!). Limited space encourages making choices and expressing them concisely. All great leaders simplify. President Ronald Reagan exhorted: 'Mr. Gorbachev, tear down that wall.' I'm sure there was more to the Cold War but on the other hand, it captured exactly what it was about (as seen through the eyes of the West).

Frequently, I'm asked about the OGSM's time frame. A strategy document typically covers the upcoming five years for most businesses. It's recommended to review the strategy at least once annually since it is an iterative process. Changes in market and economic conditions, as well as new ideas and innovations, may emerge, necessitating revision and refinement. As mentioned previously, if there is a game changer, then the strategy will require a complete re-assessment.

> **The P&G Morocco OGSM (for the sake of simplicity, Measures are not included):**
>
> <u>Objective</u>: We are 'the Mission Itspossible Team' and do things that other teams think cannot be done. We will bring the business 'From Darkness to Light' by 'Breaking the Paradox'.

Designed by Koenraad Vandewiele.

Where to Win:
1. Fix Tide – and then the laundry portfolio – as THE priority. Repeat message: Tide is THE priority.
2. Next, drive Hair Care.
   In both strategies 1. & 2., the markets and the volume are there.
3. NOT focus on driving conversion (where markets must be created) on Pampers (Baby Care) and Always (Feminine Protection) because there is no proven model at current price levels.
4. Over time, sell Comunivers and seek a cheaper distributor. But do NOT do this in the coming three to five years as the change program needs to be paced.

How to Win:
1. Majorly invest in a diverse and 'in touch' organization to drive sustainable results. Simultaneously, be tougher on performance but also ensure a much more rewarding workplace. Create a much stronger senior leadership team ASAP.
2. Take a proactive approach to managing open borders: ensure that our business is competitive to challenge and benefit from existing barriers to new entrants.
3. Win in Laundry: (a) build superiority on all product attributes, including packaging, with a focus on the suds profile, (b) fix polybags, (c) develop marketing that reflects local insights and needs, (d) massive trial events after the product is fixed and old product is removed from the shelves.
4. In Hair Care: quality improvements in the total marketing mix.
   In both strategies 3. & 4., re-establish our presence and abilities in rural areas.

5. Restore financial health: cut cost everywhere, whilst delivering quality improvements in everything we do. Build a solid 'three-legged profit stool' rather than just 'one-leg stool' Tide. Plants: 'Total Delivered Cost', quality and safety must be improved ASAP. A major restructuring, across the company, will be done to restore productivity. All product improvements must come at zero cost, ideally at lower cost.
6. Build a competitive edge at the first moment of truth (i.e. when consumers buy) via superior DPSM (Distribution, Pricing, Shelving, Merchandising). Own the High Frequency Stores.

After implementing this strategy, by mid 2004, Morocco was a successful subsidiary again: profitable (double digit growth), later with record profit and a margin equal to the Central & Eastern Europe, Middle East & Africa ('CEEMEA') regional average. Importantly, P&G retook share leadership in Laundry, which had been lost to Unilever. Tide was thriving. Hair Care shares were growing. Quality was back in all areas. On-shelf quality had improved by a factor of 16. Regretted loss was at 0%, and the subsidiary was a major exporter of talent again. Diversity was up from 15% females to 30%. Internal Controls ('IC') were under control. Morocco eventually won the global IC Award.

There's a lot more to talk about how these results were achieved beyond the strategic choices. This will be covered in some of the following chapters. You know what? *The strategy was the easy part. An OGSM is just a piece of paper with some nice words until it is delivered. The blood, sweat, and tears are in the execution of it.* The turnaround was achieved thanks to the contribution of the entire company. We had a superb local team, but it required the support of the regional and global teams to succeed. I also owe thanks to the Moroccan authorities. They understood that some very difficult decisions were required.

It was no longer in a career graveyard. I survived to run the newly acquired Gillette business for the CEEMEA region in 2005. The role was based in Geneva. That city's motto is… 'From Darkness to Light' ('Ex Tenebras Lux')!

> **EXECUTIVE SUMMARY:**
>
> 1. Via Choice Cascading, the key elements of strategy to be defined are:
>   a) the objective and aspiration;
>   b) where to play to achieve that ambition;
>   c) how to win, where one decides to play;
>   d) the capabilities required to deliver;
>   e) the management systems to support the strategic intent.
> 2. Focus on strengths and be honest about limitations.

CHAPTER 5

Do Trees Look Taller When the Grass is Cut? Defining Go-to-Market Models

≡ A critical part of the strategic exercise is to develop a Go-to-Market Model ('GMM'). A GMM details the set of differentiating activities that deliver the strategy. It describes how to create and capture value.

Let's do the exercise for Gillette in Central & Eastern Europe, Middle East & Africa ('CEEMEA'). Gillette is a fabulous and much-loved brand. As a result, in 2006, consumers rewarded its Blades and Razors ('B&R') business with an 80% share. In Russia, the most important market, it was even a 90% share. How to grow from such high levels? The strategic choice was obvious: increase CDI. That stands for Consumer Development Index. To say it in other words: focus on making the market bigger, not on share growth. Yes, that would also benefit rivals but with an 80% share, we'd get quite a slice of any bigger pie.

B&R was a very profitable business. The most important part was the 'system', consisting of a razor 'handle' on which a blade was affixed and could be replaced when blunt. 'Disposables' are the other part of the market. These are typically cheap and thrown away after a limited number of uses. Gillette's performance advantage is in systems where consumer loyalty is the highest. Disposables is very much a promotional game à la '10+5 free'. Clearly, it was to our benefit to have consumers 'trade up' into systems. See it as moving men up a ladder where the bottom rung (one bladed disposables) makes the least money and the top the most (Fusion). The Gillette razor is often promoted, offered at a low price. Blades are sold at a high price and are the ones that generate value. Once men have the razor, blades have a high chance to follow.

Just with that information, you can create a Go-to-Market Model. We called it 'the CDI wheel' (an anecdote: we had a review with the CEO. The evening before, as we reviewed our charts, the business building blocks were put in a circle. 'The CDI wheel' was born.) Where do you put your innovation? On systems obviously, less on disposables. But competition knows systems are your strength and therefore innovates in the disposables segment. Also, consider that the scale effect from the high market share is one of the reasons for Gillette's attractive profit margins. Consequently, one needs to stay competitive in disposables. A rule was set that once a new disposable segment would grow to a certain percentage of the total market (for instance the introduction of '3-bladed' disposables), Gillette would enter it as well. We preferred not to lead innovation on disposables, but we had everything ready for a fast 'from behind' introduction. We'd have offers in every segment to protect scale.

Placing razors was critical. New razors were made attractive to men by, for instance, putting the logo of their football club on the handle. In Russia, the gifting season is very important. You might not be happy to find a razor under the Xmas tree, but Russians are. It's considered 'always useful'. Hence, the CDI wheel demanded to own the gifting season. Gillette Blades & Razors had no less than three 'strategic profit control points'. The Go-to-Market Model was specifically designed to protect and/or strengthen those: (i) the market share was large; (ii) fuelled by an innovation and design lead, (iii) the brand had great loyalty because of its superior performance and 'the best a man can get' equity. There was total clarity on how money was made, and how more could be made.

In the end, with the support of the Global management team, six clear instructions were created on what the organization had to do. It drove simplification and discipline. In every business review in every country, we asked to put the CDI wheel up and to discuss the relevant blocks. It was even forbidden to change the wheel layout into a square or a triangle (knowing humanity's insatiable desire to get creative with Powerpoint). For confidentiality reasons, the 'CDI wheel' in figure 8 is mostly left empty on purpose.

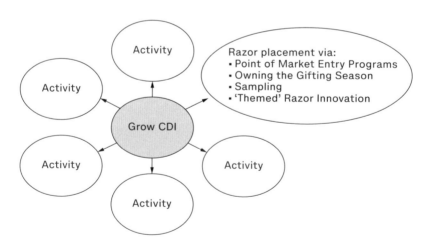

Figure 8: The Gilette Go-to-Market Model
(Source: Based on P&G CEEMEA Shave Care Model)

This Go-to-Market Model allowed us to double after-tax profits in eight years. Share grew, even in Russia. There was only one major and controversial change required to the CDI wheel during that entire time (covered in the Change Management chapter). Indeed, one of the interesting findings is that successful GMMs hardly ever change.

Some fun to end on Gillette. There was a desire to expand into body shaving to get more consumption. One ad for men had impact: 'Trees look bigger when the grass is cut.'

That Go-to-Market Models are decisive is proven by the fact that in the exact same circumstances, a different choice of activities by different companies leads to success for one and failure for the other.

It can even make the difference between life and death as in the race to be first to reach the South Pole. Part of my motivation to review this story in some detail is that several accounts have been grossly unfair to Robert Falcon Scott. Luckily, the great British polar explorer Sir Ranulph Fiennes, set the record straight in his splendid biography, 'Captain Scott'.[1]

A spoiler alert is not needed. The outcome of what happened is well known. The Norwegian Roald Amundsen reached the South Pole first on December 14, 1911. His crew made it out alive. The British Captain Scott came in second on January 17, 1912. His entire team starved on the way back. Notwithstanding this outcome, Scott's heroic pursuit has been a source of inspiration for generations, including myself. The success of Amundsen does not make Scott a hopeless bungler. Both were extraordinary, highly experienced explorers. Both reached the South Pole. Each one's approach was meticulously planned and had positives and negatives.

Amundsen relied on sledges drawn by dogs, based on knowledge gathered from the Inuit on the North Pole, and Nordic ski experience. Scott's plan was to use a pyramid approach: (i) use hardy ponies, slaughter these for meat when they could not go on anymore, (ii) use dog sledges up to the same point as the ponies (the Beardmore Glacier), (iii) then switch to manhauling with a team of 12, (iv) choose the best five for the final push to the pole. He also brought mechanized tractors as an experiment. The difference in complexity between the approaches of the two explorers is immediately apparent.

Sledge dogs offer major advantages. They can start in colder weather versus ponies. They can follow another sledge in low visibility weather conditions because they can rely on smell. There's no need to carry tents, sleeping bags and cooking utensils for them. Worst case, a dog can be slaughtered and fed to the surviving pack. They have eyelids that allow them to deal with horizontally blown snow. As a downside, they often run blindly into crevasses with catastrophic results. On the difficult terrain Scott expected, manhauling is nearly as fast.

Manhauling in general had a good rep with the Brits. It had been used with positive results during much of 19th century polar exploration. A sail was typically added to the sledge to harness wind power where possible. In modern times, kites are used. Belgian polar explorer Dixie Dansercour typically marched 20 km per day pulling a 100 kg load by manpower alone.

Ponies can handle a much heavier load than dogs. But a horse cannot eat another horse when supplies run short. As was known, they would not be able to withstand the entire journey.

The tracked vehicles were never part of the plan. They all broke down and were useless. Dixie Dansercour felt that: 'Pioneering something in those extreme conditions is a bad idea. You must rely on proven and well-tested methods only. Amundsen generally did a better job in this respect.'[2]

Captain Scott based himself on what had been the most successful trek to the South Pole to date. Earlier, Ernest Shackleton came to within 160 km of the South Pole using ponies and manhauling during the Nimrod expedition of 1909. That team wisely returned at some point because they had run out of provisions. When Mr. Shackleton explained to his wife why he turned back so close to the objective, he spoke the immortal words: 'I thought you would like a living donkey better than a dead lion.' Scott followed the route used by Shackleton and based his marching plan on the terrain encountered by the latter.

The Norwegians had two more advantages. They had chosen a landing place that was risky but nearly 100 km closer to the pole. That's a nice 200 for the total trip. They also – by sheer good fortune – chanced upon a better and faster route that gave them another 200 km round trip advantage (via the previously unknown Axel Heiberg Glacier). The Amundsen crew did an all-round magnificent job. Their journey was relatively uneventful.

Captain Scott's team died from starvation less than 20 km from a food depot on the return trip from the South Pole. It was impossible for them to move because the weather was exceptionally bad. They experienced 'freak' weather, one of the coldest streaks on record. The selfless act of team member Lawrence 'Titus' Oates did not save them. Captain Oates had a crippling foot injury. In those times, the total team would be at risk if they were slowed down by an injured man. When the remaining crew of four (the fifth, 'Taff' Evans had died earlier) were stuck in their tent because of the blizzard, running desperately low on food and fuel, Oates left the tent to die with the laconic words: 'I am just going outside and may be some time.' Sadly, his sacrifice was in vain.

Each man had opium tablets and there was a vial of morphine available to soften death. None were used. Captain Scott passed away last. When a rescue party found their remains, the others were covered with their blanket. Scott was not. His last diary entry was March 29, 1912. A cross was erected on the South Pole to honor these five valiant men. Their names are inscribed together with a verse from Alfred Lord Tennyson: 'To strive, to seek, to find and not to yield.'

The tragic fate of Scott's expedition underscores the vital importance of carefully crafting your GMM.

Amundsen also died on a polar expedition. He disappeared on June 18, 1928, while flying on a rescue mission in the Arctic. They were seeking missing members of an airship crew that had crashed, while returning from the North Pole. His body was never found. Dixie Dansercour fell to his death in a crevasse in the ice during an expedition in Greenland on June 7, 2021. He was a superb polar explorer and a wonderful man. His body could not be recovered. It's a minor consolation that Dixie rests in the landscape he loved the most on earth.

Go-to-Market Models cannot always be blindly copied in another geography. Context matters. Walmart is a case in point. Its GMM is massively successful in the USA. Yet, it has proven difficult to expand. In 2015, 80% of the overseas profits came from just three markets: Canada, Mexico and – via acquisition – the UK.[3] Here's why: building distribution and warehouses in far-flung regions delivers efficient delivery in America. But in markets without decent roads, that does not work. Integration of IT systems with small vendors allows you to share information quickly. In low-trust countries this is hard to achieve because of the existential fear that IT integration will lead to reporting to tax authorities. Big parking spaces are essential in the USA. In emerging markets, they are disliked. Simply because consumers do not have cars and may have to walk the distance in hot climates to the entrance door. In Morocco, small stores remain a big part of the distribution network because they grant credit. Supermarkets don't do that. Walmart's choice to implant superstores in rural areas was a winning strategy in the States. In Morocco, it would be a disaster because there is insufficient transport, nor is there any purchasing power. Only cities have that.

Unfortunately, once one starts to remove parts of the successful GMM, the competitive advantage disappears.

EXECUTIVE SUMMARY:

1. Go-to-Market Models turn strategy into well-defined activities.

2. It's a description of the way value is created and captured.

3. Successful Go-to-Market Models can be remarkably resilient and often require little change over time.

4. Go-to-Market Models cannot always be lifted to another market. The context may differ in another country.

CHAPTER 6

'The Power of One Dollar' to Drive Strategic Clarity in the Organization

1. 'If you only had one dollar. Who or what gets that dollar?'

Anonymously asking a company's leadership this question is a simple trick to check if the organization has strategic clarity. It is a metaphor for limited resources and the need for priority setting. You'd be surprised at the response this generates. At a $10 bn company, the 15 strong executive team gave 13 different opinions. It was all over the place: different brands, regions, projects. That's an issue. In another major multinational, young executives came up with interesting answers. There was only one problem: the CEO gave a very different one. Every employee you stop in the corridor must be able to give you the top priority mission and the core strategic focus areas.

2. It helps to have the strategy expressed in a metaphor, in one line that captures it all.

Apparently, to sell a script in Hollywood, one must be able to summarize it in one sentence (in a so-called 'logline'). Let's see if you can put the name of the film to the following.
- Great white shark creates panic in coastal town.
- Dinosaurs are genetically recreated in a tourist park but create havoc when they escape.[*]

---

[*] Jaws, Jurassic Park.

You might say: 'Oh yeah, but that's Tinseltown.' So, let's flash back to the heyday of Jack Welch's influence. Mr. Welch was the highly successful CEO of General Electric. One of his dictums was: 'Be number one or number two in your industry. If not, fix, sell or close.'[1] This left Honda's CEO puzzled. His company was nowhere near that spot in car manufacturing. The company did have a strength in small engines. Following a strategy review, they came up with the quite brilliant one-liner: 'Be number one in the garage.' It's a place full of small engines: lawn mowers, outboard engines, snow scooters, jet skis... exactly where the company's core competency lies.

3. Use inspirational language.

The Reverend Martin Luther King did not say: 'I want 2% more postal jobs for African-Americans, and a 7.5% increase in the number of accountants in government service.' No, he spoke the immortal words: 'I have a dream that one day this nation will rise up and live out the true meaning of its creed: we hold these truths to be self-evident; that all men are created equal.' Such words are certainly more memorable.

4. Set a magic goal.

The classic example is what President Kennedy asked Congress on May 25, 1961. He proposed that the USA 'should commit itself to achieving the goal, before this decade is out, of landing a man on the Moon and returning him safely to the Earth'. It galvanized the nation. On July 21, 1969, Armstrong set foot on the moon. As an eight-year-old, I vividly remember how even in my tiny village in Flanders the entire population was glued to their TV screens to see it happen. In this context it's apt to quote Leo Burnett, the legendary founder of the ad agency: 'When you reach for the stars you may not quite get one, but you won't come up with a handful of mud either.'

5. Overcommunicate.

How often do you tell your kids to look to the left and the right when crossing the street? Once? Or 100 times? It is the same with your team. The mission and the strategic priorities must be relentlessly communicated. People get so many impressions these days, from Facebook, Instagram, YouTube, that it is important to ensure enough share of voice. Chip Bergh, CEO of Levi's, shared a word of caution in this respect: 'A whisper is a storm.' That's very sound advice. Anything the leader says will be amplified and can resonate like wildfire throughout the organization. Your words matter, choose them wisely.

6. Develop an elevator speech.

A good tool in this respect is the 'message track' (see figure 9). The idea is to consistently spread the same message and to be deliberate about it. Politicians excel at it. For instance, if their program is to increase defense spending, they will turn every question to that point.

Journalist: 'What are your views on social security?'

Politician: 'It's an important area but the essential thing to fix is defense. What we want to do is increase spending by 20% because…' etc.

Just check how often an Israeli spokesperson uses the word 'terrorist' after another conflagration in the region. The Palestinian will drop in 'occupation' in just about every sentence.

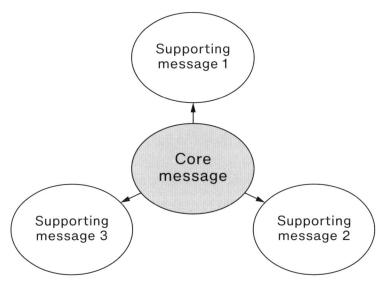

Figure 9: The Message Track (Source: P&G Media Training, Michael Sheehan)

7. **Do not overcomplicate things.**

'Miller's Law' gives us 'the magical number seven (plus or minus two)'. In short-term memory, right after one of your dazzling Powerpoint presentations, attendees will remember seven things, max. Later research suggests the following: seven for digits, six for letters, five for words. Some even find one phrase too wordy. Kevin Roberts, ex-CEO of Saatchi & Saatchi, told me that creatives were only entitled to a 'one-word equity' to describe a car model on the Toyota account. Guess what, that one strategically chosen word was enough to make some superb ads. Mr. Roberts also made the point that even individuals can be characterized by one word. Who is The Rock? The Boss? The Terminator who became the Gubernator? (For those in doubt: Dwayne Johnson, Bruce Springsteen, Arnold Schwarzenegger.) Perhaps, your team uses a word for you as well. You may want to check…

8. Bring it alive, everywhere.

> **The P&G Morocco Challenge:**
>
> We used powerful metaphors such as 'From Darkness to Light', 'To The Mountain Top' and 'Mission Itspossible'. There were cool t-shirts and bath towels with the logos. Some employees were into hip hop and produced a fantastic single called *To the Mountain Top*. It was a hit at office parties. It was great to hear people sing along with the chorus. Belgian artist, Koenraad Vandewiele, came over and painted an art route in the office that pictured the journey ahead. A lithograph was produced for everybody and much more. All that helped to restore the pride in the organization. Equally important, the strategic objectives were constantly top of mind. Nobody could say they did not know what we had to achieve.

EXECUTIVE SUMMARY:

1. Every employee must know the mission and the core strategic focus areas.
2. These are constantly communicated in inspirational words and images.
3. Set a magic goal.
4. Overcommunicate.
5. Develop an elevator speech.
6. Do not overcomplicate things.
7. Bring it alive, everywhere.

B.
PERFECT EXECUTION

CHAPTER 7

Lessons from Alice Cooper, Napoleon and Hannibal

The following two chapters will focus on achieving Perfect Execution. This first chapter will cover the fundamental concepts, while the subsequent chapter will provide specific tools and techniques to accomplish this goal.

Here's a compelling case of successfully translating strategy into effective execution. In the 1970s, manager Shep Gordon adopted a simple approach for rock band Alice Cooper: 'If parents hate the band, kids will love them.' The question then becomes, how did he put this plan into action? Mr. Gordon came up with the idea to wrap women's panties around the vinyl in the packaging of Alice's 1972 *School's Out* album. He was certain this would upset parents, whereas many 17-year-olds would adore it. One day, he read an article about a shipment of paper panties that was confiscated by U.S. Customs because of a Flammable Fabrics Act violation. That account provided the inspiration. He then played tactics by making two orders for these paper knickers. One order of panties had goods that were on standard for use on the record sleeve.

Another small order was not on standard. He called a friendly journalist at the Washington Post and briefed him that this off-standard shipment would be seized by Customs. The journalist duly followed-up and published a page-one article headlined *Largest Panty Raid in History*. It explained that Alice Cooper's album was going to be packaged in them. Lots of other newspapers picked it up. Parents read the story over breakfast and were surely scandalized. Teenagers were not. The *School's Out* album was a major success, hitting number two in the US charts.[1]

- A definition of Execution: Execution is a system for getting things done. It fuses strategy with the market and organizational reality. It's a device for accomplishing an end; a method of employing resources in a certain market situation.

- Tactics are part of execution. These are planned and ad hoc activities meant to deal with the demands of the moment, and to move from one milestone to another in pursuit of the overall strategic goal(s).

No consumer is interested in what your strategy document says. Anyway, it's mostly written in 'corporatese', that strange language full of three letter acronyms (GMM, MSE, BSA, BUE…) only insiders understand. Yes, people care about your purpose and values. Nobody likes to buy clothes made by child labour. But other than that, what matters is the value your products or services deliver. Execution is vastly underrated. Do a test: type in 'Business Strategy' in the books section of Amazon.co.uk. You'll get >60,000 suggestions. Now do the same for 'Business Execution'. >3000 options are offered, or 5% of the strategy yield. That's not the right ratio. Strategy matters but must always be turned into value creating execution. Insight without action is worthless.

1. **Strategy means little if the execution is flawed.**

The cautionary tale of Napoleon Bonaparte at Waterloo highlights the perils of sound strategy executed poorly, underscoring the need for leaders to apply the same level of meticulousness to execution as they do to strategy. It demonstrates that even a strategic mastermind can lose everything due to poor execution.

Going into the campaign, Bonaparte faced a near impossible challenge. He was assured of the loyalty of his 123,000 strong army. Many were veterans of tough campaigns. The elite Imperial Guard was a mythical regiment and reputed to be unbeatable. But the odds were not in his favour. Everybody in Europe had mobilized against his regime. Austria, Russia, the restored Netherlands, Prussia, and Britain, together with the displaced monarchist French regime, agreed at the Congress of Vienna to destroy Napoleon once and for all. Their efforts would culminate in Waterloo. Across the French frontier, two of their armies were already present in Belgium, albeit in different parts of the country. Further away, two more vast armies were being readied to join the fight. The only option for Bonaparte was to pro-actively go on the offensive and try to defeat each army in turn before they could combine forces. That was what he set out to do.

In other countries	Austria: 150,000	Russia: 200,000
Belgium	Britain: 92,000	Prussia: 130,000
France	Napoleon's Forces: 123,000	

In the end, Napoleon lost at Waterloo, not on that Sunday June 18, 1815, but two days earlier by a series of executional blunders. It's a mystery how so many experienced French commanders could perform as poorly as they did. The strategy to tackle each army in turn was sound enough. The Prussians (under Marshall Gebhard Leberecht Blücher) and the Brits (under Arthur Wellesley, first Duke of Wellington) were camped in different parts of Belgium. Napoleon would engage the Prussians first. However, it was critical to ensure that the British could not come to their rescue. This could be guaranteed by taking the Quatre Bras crossroads, 32 km to the south of Brussels, controlling the Charleroi – Brussels highway. All alternative roads were but twisting country lanes and obstructed by narrow bridges, virtually unpassable for an army on the march. That junction was the hinge between the two Allied armies.

Marshall Ney was ordered to secure Quatre Bras on the dawn of June 16. At the time, the crossroads was but lightly defended by 4,000 undersupplied men. Inexplicably, Ney did nothing. Napoleon's plan was to take on the Prussians at Ligny. With the crossroads secured, Ney would then march back and fall like a hammer blow upon the Prussians' right. By the time Marshal Ney finally did act, the Quatre Bras area had been massively re-enforced by Wellington. A full-scale battle ensued, and Ney was stuck. It cost Napoleon the decisive victory at Ligny. The French army did win but fell short of the objective to annihilate the Prussian army. The latter regrouped, and eventually came to support the British army in Waterloo to give Bonaparte the coup de grâce. Napoleon mistakenly believed the Prussians could not join for another two days.

The list of inexplicable communication, command and tactical errors goes on. A force of 33,000 under Marshal de Grouchy had been dispatched belatedly to pursue the Prussians after Ligny, whilst the emperor moved against Wellington. Napoleon went against his own wise maxim: 'No force should be detached on the eve of battle, because affairs may change during the night, either by the retreat of the enemy, or the arrival of large reinforcements which might enable him to resume the offensive and render your previous dispositions disastrous.'[2] Grouchy achieved little. He did not catch the Prussian main force. Though he heard the guns of Waterloo, he never came to Napoleon's aid. Bonaparte allowed Wellington to choose the field of battle, though another of his maxims was never to do what the enemy wishes done, 'a field of battle, therefore, which he has previously studied and reconnoitred should be avoided.'[3]

Certainly, Napoleon underestimated Wellington. He dismissively called him a 'sepoy-General'. The duke had started his career in India. Wellington had mauled several French armies earlier in Portugal and Spain, marching his victorious army into France up to Toulouse. Still, he was lowly rated by the emperor **(never underestimate a competitor)**. Following this defeat, the French emperor was forced to abdicate again, sent to exile to St. Helena where he died on May 5, 1821.[4]

2. High performing organizations sweat the small stuff.

When I visited McLaren's Formula 1 Team in the UK and attended backstage operations at several Grand Prix, I noticed that everything was kept spotlessly clean. One could literally eat off the floor. I had expected a garage to be a bit smutty. I asked why they seemed so concerned about cleanliness. There was a strong executional reason. If an oil drop is found on the floor and there is no discipline, then that drop can come from a lot of sources. Maybe a mechanic had spilled it, maybe a bottle had not been sealed properly, or a cleaning team had not done a good enough job. If everything is kept pristine, the drop can come from one place only: the car engine. Obviously, it's important to spot an engine problem fast in Formula 1. Explorer Dixie Dansercour gave me a surprising answer when I asked him what he valued the most in team members. He said: 'Attention to detail.' Indeed, the more VUCA the environment (such as the Poles), the more minor mistakes can have dramatic consequences.

Great leaders see the big picture but equally take notice of small details that can make the difference between success and failure, as we'll see in Operation White Angels. Sabena airlines flight 571, en route to Tel Aviv, was going smoothly until it was over Yugoslavia. Suddenly, pilot Reginald Levy felt the cold steel of a pistol in his neck. The plane was hijacked by two men and two women. They belonged to Black September; a new terrorist organization secretly created by Yasser Arafat. Captain Levy was ordered to continue the course to Lod airport (now Ben Gurion) in Tel Aviv. Once landed, the terrorist leader, Captain Rif'at communicated his demands. Israel was to release 317 Palestinians held in its jails and fly them to Cairo. Upon hearing confirmation of their safe arrival there, the Sabena flight was to proceed to the Egyptian capital as well. All hostages would then be released. If Black September did not get what they asked for, they'd blow up the entire plane with all inside.

The Israelis played for time. They had no intention to give in to the demands. Sayaret Matkal, the best commando team of the IDF, was called in. It was led by Colonel Ehud Barak, the future Prime Minister. The first thing that needed to be done was to immobilize the plane. As night fell on that May day in 1972, daredevil Barak with one other soldier and a veteran airplane mechanic crawled under the aircraft's belly. They removed the valve controlling the hydraulic system of the landing gear. Captain Levy saw the hydraulic oil warning light and reported the problems to the control towers and the terrorists. They agreed to allow a repair team to approach the plane. The mechanics sent were 16 Sayaret commandos (one of them was the future Prime Minister Benjamin 'Bibi' Netanyahu).

Now it gets interesting. For the ruse to work, the commandos donned white overalls, brought over from a nearby hospital. But General Rehavam Ze'evi stopped them. He noticed that the overalls looked too white, too immaculate. The soldiers were asked to soil and crumple their overalls, so they'd look the part. Ze'evi stopped them again. The commandos were all young and superbly fit. No crew of mechanics could possibly be that ripped. It would arouse suspicion. Some older men were added. The devil is in the details, even for white angels. The attack started at 4.24p.m. In only 90 seconds, it was over. Sadly, one passenger was mortally wounded during the take-over. All other passengers were safe (we will return to this raid as there are more lessons in it).[5]

3. Be aware that seemingly insignificant factors can significantly impact outcomes.

One of my favourite stories in this regard comes from Malcolm Gladwell's *The Tipping Point*.[6] Two Princeton University psychologists decided to conduct a study based on the biblical story of the Good Samaritan. For the benefit of those of you who were asleep during Bible class: this New Testament story recounts how a man was robbed and left for dead by the side of the road from Jerusalem to Jericho. Two supposedly virtuous men, a priest, and a Levite, passed him by and did nothing. The only one to help was a Samaritan. In those days, Samaritans and Jews did not get along. The former were a disliked minority based on theological disputes, one being that Samaritans claimed that their – and only their – copy of the Pentateuch was the original and true one. They dismissed that Jerusalem was holy and scorned anything written since Moses.[7] To say that Samaritans were unpopular is putting it mildly.

It was decided to replicate this event at the Princeton Theological Seminary. A group of seminarians was individually briefed to prepare a talk on a biblical theme and walk to a nearby building to present it. On the way to that presentation, they would encounter a groaning man, lying down and clearly in distress. Three variables were introduced into the experiment:
a) Students had to make a choice on why they had chosen theology as a field of study. Was it for personal spiritual fulfilment or a practical tool for finding meaning in everyday life?
b) The theme for the presentation was varied. Some were given the parable of the Good Samaritan.

c) Some students were told they were late for their presentation and that they had to hurry. Others were encouraged to get moving but assured that there was plenty of time.

From the list above, the only thing which had an impact was time pressure. Only 10% of those who were late stopped to help. 63% of those with time to spare intervened. Just that one phrase 'you're late' made some compassionate and others not. This finding is totally accurate, as we know all too well when we have to drive to an important event but are running late. Road rage has a lot to do with time pressure. Workers on road repairs – that inevitably cause delays – report lots of insults by passing drivers.

4. Behavior is often a function of social context. Therefore, manage the context.

People who get fined by the police for minor stuff, often tell them in strongly worded terms that they should focus on capturing thieves and killers, not small offenders like them. That sentiment is wrong. We know from 'the broken windows' theory that a crackdown on quality-of-life transgressions leads to lower serious crimes. New York successfully put the theory into action to tackle the crime epidemic of the late 80s and early 90s. Criminologists James Q. Wilson and George Kelling argued that crime is the consequence of disorder. If a building is left in a sorry state with a window broken, people conclude that nobody cares. Before one knows it, more windows get smashed. Like a rotten tooth, the decayed building starts to infect a whole neighborhood. The experience in the Underground is similar. Once one seat is torn in a carriage, people get into some sort of frenzy and soon the entire carriage is vandalized. People find joy in creating but equally in destruction, it seems. When the police started to act against graffiti, panhandlers, squeezy boys and garbage, 'serious' crime decreased significantly.[8]

The P&G Morocco Challenge – improving the context:

One of the reasons, we believed, that product quality was below par was a run-down infrastructure. Though we had serious profit challenges, half a million dollars was immediately invested in clean-ups, refurbishing, new toilets and showers. Every time we visited an office, the management team would personally control the restrooms, check if all was in order, even ask to put on every single light to check that no lamp was broken. Any issue spotted had to be promptly repaired within a week and pictures sent as proof. Employee safety was tackled. For instance, new cars were bought for the sales force to replace the dangerous lemons they drove. *The single most important duty of a leader is to ensure that people go back safe and sound to their families at the end of the day.*

In the plant, the initial manager's office had paint peeling off the wall. The excuse was cost savings and therefore 'this office should be the last one to be painted'. That office had to be the first one to be repainted! *The leader sets the standard.* One cannot expect people to be all meticulous about their work when all around them they see the opposite.

Running ahead of a later chapter, such measures have one other important benefit: early wins. When somebody expressed doubts that we were serious about change, I'd ask: 'Did you go to the toilet recently? Was it different? Things are going to change around here!'

5. To be tactically sound but strategically weak is obviously bad too.

A prime example of this scenario is the legendary battle between Hannibal and Rome. Hannibal Barca (247–between 183 and 181 BC) was a Carthaginian general and statesman who commanded Carthage's main forces against the Roman Republic during the Second Punic War. He had daringly crossed the Alps with his elephants and army into Italy in 218 BC. Hannibal was a masterly leader and as shrewd a fellow as ever commanded an army. He was the very incarnation of Sun Tzu's belief that all warfare is based on deception.

In 216 BC, the Romans decided it was time to deal with the Carthaginian threat once and for all. A massive 87,000 strong army was mustered. Hannibal had 50,000 troops at his disposal. The Romans however made one critical mistake. They divided the leadership between two consuls, Varro and Paullus. They were like oil and water when it came to strategy. Varro was impulsive and eager to get straight into the fight. Paullus was cautious. His strategy was based on patience, containment, and starvation of the invaders. According to the Roman historian Livy,[9] Paullus argued that Hannibal's army could only live off the land and would ultimately find resources scarce. Since the two consuls could not agree, it was foolishly decided that they alternate command every other day (*shared authority is usually a recipe for disaster*).

At Cannae, Hannibal lured the Romans into a trap. He set up his army with his weakest troops in the centre and the strongest at the flanks. As the Romans charged, they successfully fought their way through the middle. But as they advanced the front became U-shaped until Hannibal could close the jaws and surround them. He also had 500 men feign surrender. They hid their weapons. Eventually, they attacked the Roman rear which created further havoc in the Roman ranks. It was a massacre. At least 50,000 legionnaires were killed. Consul Paullus refused to flee when offered the gift of a fast horse and was slain. Hothead Varro survived.

Now Hannibal's strategic weakness came to the fore. After the fight, his army took a rest and celebrated the victory. Livy recounts how Maharbal, the commander of his cavalry, was convinced that there was not a moment to be lost.

'Sir,' he said, 'if you want to know the true significance of this battle, let me tell you that within five days you will take your dinner, in triumph, on the Capitol. I will go first with my horsemen. The first knowledge of our coming will be the sight of us at the gates of Rome. You have but to follow.'

Maharbal was right: *when a competitive advantage is gained, it is crucial to pursue it relentlessly and swiftly.* Hannibal wavered and answered that he needed to think things over. 'Assuredly,' Maharbal replied, 'no man has been blessed with all God's gifts. You know, Hannibal, how to win a fight; you do not know how to use your victory.'

The Romans believed that that day's delay was the salvation of the city and the Empire. For a short while, they were utterly defenceless. Hannibal lost more time and sent envoys to negotiate terms. To his surprise, the Roman Senate even refused to talk and declared that they would never surrender. They would prove true to their word. It took another 14 years of struggle, but they would destroy Carthage (in today's Tunisia) in 202 BC. The Carthaginian general underestimated the resilience of the Romans. He also failed to realize that the city of Rome was the central nerve centre. Capturing and destroying that power base was the only right plan. ***Identifying the appropriate strategic objective is essential.***

6. There is no dichotomy between strategy and execution. They are intrinsically linked.

It reminds me of the discussions about 'nature or nurture' to analyse people's behaviour, 'heart or brain' when making a career choice. Both should be considered of course. The notion that some employees should be strategic and others executional should be firmly rejected. All have both roles, albeit at different levels. Every salesperson must be strategic in the sense that they need to list the right power SKUs (Stock Keeping Units) and drive the in-store execution that maximizes profit and market share. A CEO needs to follow up on execution. This is not the same as micromanagement.

One of the greatest ancient historians, Thucydides (460–400 BC), covered the war between Athens and Sparta. A Spartan King was recorded as saying that a nation that makes a distinction between thinkers and fighters, ends up with the thinking done by cowards and the fighting by fools.* Provocative words, no doubt. But the underlying thought has merit. The CEO has the helicopter view but lacks contact with the

---

*   Sparta won.

frontline. The frontline sees customers every day but may not have the overview. Both levels have unique advantages that must be combined and exploited (this will be achieved via the Lean Organism Management Model, covered in the very last chapter).

First, let's answer the question: if execution matters that much, what tools can we use to make it better.

> **EXECUTIVE SUMMARY:**
>
> 1. Execution is a system for getting things done; it meshes strategy with reality.
> 2. Great organizations and leaders get involved in execution.
> 3. Context influences behaviour. Perfect execution is stimulated by a perfect environment.
> 4. Small things often have big outcomes.
> 5. There is no dichotomy between strategy and execution. All employees must do both.

CHAPTER 8

'Do You Want Teddy Bears or Top Pilots?' Practical Ways to Improve Execution

1. **Create Current Best Approaches ('CBA') plus a feedback loop with After Action Reviews ('AAR') and continuous testing.**

In the Gillette Blades and Razors Go-to-Market Model, it was mentioned that 'winning the gifting season' was important. However, that is insufficient to achieve perfect execution. One must then create a CBA as guidance. These are constantly updated with new learning.

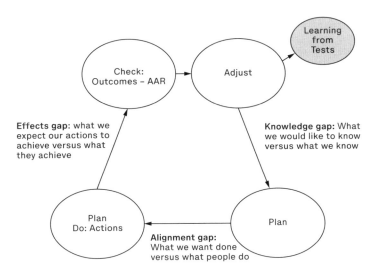

Figure 10: The CBA Loop
(Source: Gaps: Dialogos Seminar, PDCA model: Dr. W.E. Deming)

Let's illustrate how a CBA takes shape. Normally, men buy their shaving products. But during the Xmas gifting season, it's women who purchase them. They are often less familiar with the category. Hence, more education on-shelf and on the packaging is important. We also thought it would be a good idea to air an emotional piece of advertising to support the drive. Basically: man opens Xmas package, finds Gillette, is happy, kisses wife, love all around. But after one season, we've learned that Russian women did not care much about that. What they wanted was reassurance that they bought the best stuff around so their husband would be happy to receive great gear. (Men and their gear, an enduring love affair! Why? Because gear is an extension of the male ego.) Does one need a promotion on these gift packs? We thought that nice gift packaging would suffice. However, we quickly learned that a promotion was needed. Yet, who wants to receive a gift that says '20% off' or 'second at half price?' Any promotional sticker had to be easily removable, even stating 'pull this corner to remove'.

CBAs must be broadly communicated, 'down to the cleaner'. Giving all the above information to a new Gillette manager would equip him or her much better than merely stating: 'go and win the gifting season'. One Unilever CEO once lamented: 'If only Unilever knew what it knows.' Therefore, ensure there is a process to communicate the CBAs to the relevant parts of the organization.

CBAs do not mean inflexibility. For instance, we also had a CBA for Point of Market Entry programs ('POME'). This means introducing boys and men to the benefits of Gillette at moments when they were most open to evaluate their brand choices.

Israel has the army draft at 18. That's when we would sample young men with Gillette. Most countries don't have a draft. Hence, we do it at other moments. Some countries allow to talk to 14-year-old boys in school, others don't. What's important is that every market had a POME program, based on what could be achieved locally. We would still develop a CBA for the different approaches because some of the insights were universal.

Let's do a fun quiz:
- What is important to 14-year-olds?
- What would your message be to students in their last year at university? Would it be different?

As a teenager, you may have told your parents how deeply you cared about your school results, but in reality, your primary concern was to be attractive. Consequently, Gillette offered grooming advice to help young boys feel more handsome. At 22, priorities have already changed somewhat. Graduating students worry about landing their first job. Therefore, the message shifted to providing confidence in job interviews ('put your best face forward').

Constant testing of other executions to improve the CBA is important. The idea is to always have small, low risk tests around executional elements. As an example: could we build the Gillette brand or parts of it by using non-TV media only? By using digital only? Learnings then help to upgrade the media CBA. Durk Jager, the ex-CEO of P&G had an excellent motto: 'test a little, spend a little, learn a lot!'

The 'After Action Review' ('AAR'), the check of outcomes, is another key tool to create a permanent positive feedback loop. The analysis' conclusions allow to adjust the CBA. If hindsight is 200% accurate, let's at least get the learning from it. After Action Reviews work if there are four key ingredients:
a. Actions and results are monitored.
b. It's not a blame game. It's about learning and improvement.
c. There is a culture of candid feedback, of positive conflict.
d. Closure is reached.

I decided to go visit the Israeli Airforce to learn about how they conduct an AAR. They allowed me to sit in for part of the meeting and to visit some of their facilities. Every jet flight is carefully monitored and videotaped. Upon return to base, the pilots gather for an AAR. The first question that was asked struck me: 'Hey, who has a really bad video?' Let's face it, in many companies that would be the last video to be shown. Or it would never see the light of day. ('My camera did not work properly today'.) There's focus on a bad video because more can be learned from it than from a video where all went perfectly well. Certainly, the price for failure in an Air Force is very high. A jet is a killing machine. Bombing a school instead of a legitimate target is not only tragic in terms of loss of innocent life but also a PR disaster.

The commanding officer often shows his video first. That's leadership by example. The comments made on a video are not taken personally. The sole focus is on how to better succeed the mission (of course, if one shows bad performance after bad performance, eventually it will get noticed). Closure is provided by drawing conclusions from the debate. When I asked how the organization deals with harsh criticisms, a question was shot back: 'What do you want? The best fighter pilots or teddy bears?' Being able to take candid feedback was rated as one of the key personality traits they look for. No matter what somebody's abilities are, if they cannot take the punches of blunt feedback, they are weeded out.

In an AAR, one can identify three possible execution gaps, and make appropriate adjustments:
a. The knowledge gap: as we make a new plan, what did we miss in terms of knowledge? What do we need to learn?
b. The alignment gap: why did people not deliver the actions from the plan?
c. The effects gap: why did the actions not result in what we aimed for?[1]

That a culture of constructive criticism matters was proven by Reckitt-Benckiser's ('RB') Bart Becht, CEO from 1995 to 2011. He increased the market cap by a whopping 500%. That's a stellar performance for a company that sells soap. RB believes positive conflict was a key success driver. Importantly, it worked because of clear ground rules:
- Show up to every meeting 100% prepared.
- Craft an opinion and deliver it with conviction (and data).
- Stay open to others' ideas, not just your own.
- Let the best argument win, even if it isn't yours (and often it isn't).
- Feel free to stand up and shout, but never make the argument personal.
- Always listen – really listen – to minority views.
- Never pursue consensus for its own sake.

These rules are important because a fight can also get out of hand. It can result in bitter animosity, hatred and outright anarchy. Management Professor Morten T. Hansen provides a helpful table (figure 11).[2] One wants to be in the top right quadrant: have open and honest discussions but maintain the team spirit. Israel's 'Start-Up Nation' economic miracle owes a lot to its ability to fight and unite in business.[3] Do note that candidness does not mean one has to be a jerk. For instance, employees can be told that they are not performing well in a respectful way.

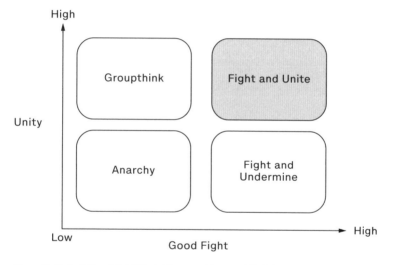

Figure 11: Unity & Good Fight Model (Source: 'Great at Work. How Top Performers Do Less, Work Better, and Achieve More', by Morten T. Hansen.)

What if you do not have the right culture? How to change culture? It's covered in Pillar 4.

2. Never get into something unless you can sustain it.

In the late 90s, P&G wanted to change trade terms drastically in France and Germany, both core markets. The trade disagreed and responded by delisting P&G brands. Volume tanked. Rightly or wrongly, P&G folded because these losses could not be sustained.

British General (ret.) Sir Rupert Smith calls out five critical factors in handling a force in figure 12 below.[4] Regarding executional excellence, it's worthwhile to share them. An important one is *not starting something one cannot get out of*. For instance, it's easy to get into a price war but devilishly tricky to get out of them. All the more reason to be wary of the 'macho school of business' ('let's teach them a lesson!').

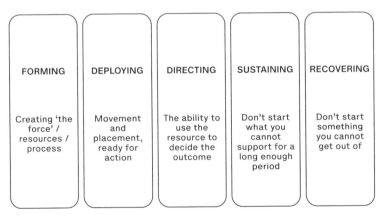

Figure 12: Strategy Into Action: 5 Critical Factors
(Source: General Sir Rupert Smith, 'The Utility of Force')

3. A process to drive executional excellence may be needed.

> **The P&G Morocco Challenge - in search of excellence:**
>
> Quality was at unacceptable levels, across the board. That is an important insight. It means that the issue was systemic and not topical. It was not just one person who did not deliver. There had to be a root cause. Certainly, we worked the culture, but that was not enough. Just telling people to 'try harder' was not going to cut it. Analysis showed that the weaknesses were related to areas that involved a 'chain of activities'.
>
> Let's take the settling of an invoice as an example. Improving our payment record was essential. Suppliers had experience of very long delays to get paid. They therefore increased their prices to cover the financing cost. We badly needed lower costs. For payments to run smoothly, there are several steps required in the procedure. A purchase order must be issued, a different person receives the goods, another person approves the invoice, and it goes to yet another person to ensure it is paid by the bank. The supplier must be registered properly. We often had glitches in the links of such chains. There was a need for a Six Sigma type of process to tackle the quality issues. Six Sigma is a system of management techniques that allows you to improve business processes by reducing errors and defects, or the probability of them.
>
> We called it 'ISO-X', short for 'In Search of Excellence'. We set up ten teams around ten key processes that needed

better execution. Importantly, we asked those who had to manage the process to come up with the solutions. One of my maxims is that the people who recommend the change must be the ones who have to live with the consequences of their choices. Progress was reviewed each month in the executive meeting. A detailed scorecard was kept. In a short period of time, quality improved.

4. Always explain the WHY.

One of the key findings of spending time with Navy SEALs, anti-terror commandos, and paratroopers was that they have very detailed CBAs. In training the 'why' is consistently provided for each element and relentlessly repeated. For instance, when parachuting, why get out of your parachute just before landing in the sea? Because, the chute will take water and drag you down with it if you are stuck in your harness. Why, on landing in a field, immediately move quickly to stand against the wind? Because otherwise your chute will catch wind and drag you along.

5. At time of strategy, it's ok to have doubts, but at the time of execution one must act with total conviction.

I was 17 and horribly airsick in the shaking C-130 Hercules plane. To my embarrassment, I had already puked up most of my breakfast. When the side door of the plane was opened, I welcomed the gusts of air and the prospect that I would be ordered to jump out shortly. I was with 80 other boys who had been given the chance to train for two weeks with Belgium's elite regiment, the 'red beret' para-commando regiment. After the order was given to the first boy in the row to 'stand in the door', the alarm went off and we swiftly moved like a well trained machine to the exit. There was no room for hesitation. It was time to jump. In Krav Maga, the motto is 'what comes out comes out.' Once you are engaged to stop an attack, there can be no doubts, if you screw up the technique, no problem, keep going, never stop until the mission is completed. ***Conviction comes from capabilities***. It's up next.

EXECUTIVE SUMMARY:

1. Current Best Approaches ('CBA'), and a feedback loop with After Action Reviews and continuous testing to drive executional excellence.
2. Never start something you cannot sustain, or you cannot get out of.
3. You may need to install a process to drive executional excellence.
4. Always explain WHY the CBA makes sense.
5. At time of strategy have doubts, but at time of execution be totally convinced.

C.
CAPABILITIES

CHAPTER 9

Learning Plans, Microbattles & Why Leaders Must Be Readers

The third component of the Mission Success Equation involves building Capabilities. Dreams can be infinite, resources never are. The 'what we want done' and 'what we can do' must ultimately be aligned. If there are gaps, they must be closed by either reducing objectives or enhancing capabilities.

1. **Strategy must always be checked versus the available means and capabilities.**

At Gillette CEEMEA, we wanted to get closer to the local consumer. Russian, Arab and Turkish men do differ from those in Southern California. Because the brand was historically very centrally led, the capability to discover local consumer insights was less developed. In other words, CEEMEA's market research capabilities had to be strengthened. That costs money. Equally, regional Ad Agency capability had to be increased. The investment into local insights allowed to develop and exploit a concept adored by Russian men: 'Reveal your inner steel.' It featured ice-hockey player

Alexandr Ovetsjkin training in the cold of winter, taking a dive into freezing water and showing determination on the playing field. But the ad could only be made because the required capabilities mentioned above had been built.

The available capabilities also answer the question on whether it is better to engage at a very specific point in depth or on a wider front against competition. It very much depends on your resources. If you have lots to spare and rivals do not, then a broad engagement can make imminent sense. The American Civil War (1861–1865) is a good example in this respect. The North had vastly greater resources than the Confederate South. Yet the South was holding out. A genius leader like President Lincoln grasped the implication in terms of grand strategy already in 1861. In his own words:

> *'I state my general idea of this war that we have the greater numbers and the enemy has the greater facility of concentrating forces upon points of collision (because of his interior lines); that we must fail unless we can find some way of making our advantage an over-match for his; and that this can only be done by menacing him at different points, at the same time; so that we can safely attack, one, or both, if he makes no change; and if he weakens one to strengthen the other, forebear to attack the strengthened one, but seize, and hold the weakened one, gaining so much.'*[1]

If one only has limited resources, then it is best to concentrate all efforts in one point – a '*Schwerpunkt*' – where competitive advantage can be created.

2. **It is totally acceptable to identify a strategic 'where to win' area even if one does not yet know how to win, provided a 'Microbattle' plan is designed at lower risk and scale.**

This is a concept very much favoured by Bain Consulting. It is inevitable that there will be areas where one has no experience yet. If China is a geography critical for the company, but there is no capability in that market, a microbattle is declared. To just enter the country without proper experience might be costly and possibly fatal. Better to assign a team which gets the mission to teach the company how to win in China at low risk. For instance, this could be done via a series of smaller market or city tests. Note that a Microbattle is not the same as just some testing. It is a must-win battle, a must-learn. The list of Microbattles is approved by the executive team and is reviewed each month. They are that important for strategic success.

STRATEGY	MICROBATTLE	WHO / WHAT	BY WHEN	KPIs
Taken from company / division strategy	Define must win	Resources and Team	Agreed timing	What does success look like?

Figure 13: Microbattle Mapping
(© 2017 Peter Corijn / VUCASTAR; inspired by a Bain Consulting concept)

3. **Competence leads to confidence. It's not the other way around. Competence comes from capabilities.**

Earlier it was said that hope is not a strategy. However, that does not mean that hope has no role to play. It does matter if we define it as the conviction of the organization that things can and will get better. The more skilled people are, the more they feel up to the job and the stronger their belief that the mission is possible. When asked whether ambition was detrimental due to the frustration it may cause, the Indian spiritual leader Sadhguru responded that ambition itself is not problematic. The issue is that ambition frequently stems from desire, rather than competence. His sage advice was to maintain an unwavering focus on developing the latter.

4. **Achieving mastery drives inherent motivation.**

Mastery is a great source of pride, whether one excells at a sport or a craft.

5. **Relentlessly build the capabilities of the organization. The most important resource is human. So, let's strengthen its muscle.**

Every department should define their respective needs. For instance, if there is an expectation that digital experience will grow in importance, it should be recognized and a corresponding learning plan should be created. In the end, the process results in an individualized learning plan for each employee as per figure 14. This has a twofold objective:
- It allows the individual to develop strengths and improve on areas of opportunity.

- It incorporates the domains where the company decided to develop skills to achieve the strategic objective.

It's recommended to put it into a process via defining Objective, specific Actions and Key Performance Indicators ('KPIs'). Every six months, the supervising manager reviews progress with the employee. A colour coding is applied: red/amber/green. Learning can take place in many ways. The most important one is the on-the-job one. That easily accounts for 70%. However, there is also outside learning, for instance an executive course at a business school. Some people may benefit from a mentor, others from a coach. A mentor takes a more holistic view, whereas a coach is performance driven.

	OUTSIDE	SELF-LEARNING	ON THE JOB	COACHING	MENTORING
Objective	Master digital transformation	Read on digital transformation	E-commerce transformation	Become better at written presentations	Struggling with company culture
Actions	Follow the IMD course	Read 'The Digital Vortex'	Become part of project team	Get expert coach	Ask CMO to mentor
KPIs	Sign up March session	1 book before IMD course	Meeting with CEO by Feb	By mid-Feb: OK to funding	Set up lunch in January
Status: Red / Amber / Green	Red. Chase budget	Green	Amber. No OK yet	Red. Not approved	Green. Done

Figure 14: Learning Plan: example on learning about digital
(© 2017 Peter Corijn / VUCASTAR)

6. You cannot blame people for not knowing what they don't know.

The Moroccan organization was very young, with an average of only 18 months seniority. On top, there had not been sufficient investment into people development. An anecdote: at some point a delegation of managers came to my office. They said: 'Peter, we do not understand you. You talk about inflection points, choice cascading, barriers to entry, profit zoning. We simply have no clue what you mean.' So, we aimed to have the best training program in the world, bar none. If somebody would find a better one, we'd increase our investment. Regretfully, as you know from the case, we did not exactly have the funds to send everybody to Harvard. We came up with 'Knowledge Miles'. It worked like an airline loyalty program. The basic level was gold. If we hit our targets, we'd put more funds into development to make it platinum. Individuals achieving a stretch goal got to diamond. They got a ticket to London with one condition: come back with a piece of knowledge to share.

It does not have to cost fortunes. The total cost of the program was only $50k per year. I realized that a lot of my friends were by now senior business leaders somewhere as well. So, I called them: 'Isn't it time for a romantic weekend for you and your partner? I'll pay for your tickets and trip to Marrakech but there's one condition:

you have to deliver a one-day business training. You can choose the topic as long as it is case study oriented and provides support for the P&G Morocco mission.' That was done every quarter. Many friends took up the offer. To save cost, we often lodged them at my house when in Casablanca. We also had inspirational leaders such as Robert A. McDonald and Kevin Roberts over.

7. **Inspiration can come from anywhere, but it must come from somewhere.**

Every meeting room was provided with a piece of inspiration ('Inspirational Pit Stop'). It costs nothing to paint a wall in the white/red chequered motif of Tintin's rocket to the moon and to make Tintin's albums available. Another room had the RAF cocarde. That was used by the Mods (a music genre and youth subculture from the sixties in the UK). The Kinks and The Who albums could be picked up. One business book was offered every quarter. We installed the 'Treasure Box', a pirate treasure chest where employees could find copies of Business Week and Fortune.

To get closer to local community leaders, 'U.F.O. Maroc' was created. This stands for U Forum on Morocco. The meeting room layout was in a U. Every quarter for two hours, managers could meet local decision makers. For instance, the governor of Casablanca, the US ambassador, a Board member of the biggest local holding. It had another advantage. Afterwards, I had

lunch with these people and could suggest some actions that would benefit the company (otherwise known as 'lobbying').

We never forced anybody to attend or to read anything. It was all voluntary (note: the personal learning plans were not). Events were always oversubscribed.

8. **Personal development is the responsibility of the employee. But the leader must create the conditions into which learning can take place.**

9. **Leaders should be readers.**

Reading is an essential part of leadership development. Here's why:

a) It gives extra experience at zero risk.

Nobody put it better than General (ret.) Mattis, in his autobiography *Call Sign Chaos*. He led the US Marines and was Secretary of Defence in the US government:

> *'If you haven't read hundreds of books, you are functionally illiterate, and you will be incompetent, because your personal experiences alone aren't broad enough to sustain you. Any commander who claims he is "too busy to read" is going to fill body bags with his troops as he learns the hard way. Reading sheds light on the hard road ahead.'*[2]

A history professor once said that we can learn in two ways: by putting our hand on a red-hot stove or by listening to people who have done it before us.³ You can read in a week what took a given author 30 years of experience and effort to discover. A nice side benefit is that you can learn about others' failures at zero risk. Biographies are particularly insightful in this respect. As Chancellor Otto von Bismarck once remarked: 'Only a fool learns from his own mistakes. The wise man learns from the mistakes of others.' Define an expert! Most people answer: 'Somebody who knows everything about a given topic'. No, an expert is somebody who knows more than you. I'm willing to wager that if you read ten books on a certain business topic, you will already know more than many of your competitors. That knowledge can help you and your team to succeed.

b) It provides 'range'.

Increasingly, there is evidence that generalists do better than specialists in areas that are unpredictable and complex (as business is). They are more creative, more agile, and able to make connections their more specialized peers can't see. Anything can provide inspiration, a book on Darwinism, on ancient Sparta, or a detective story. Creativity is about making new connections between knowledge blocks that spark insight. So, the more knowledge blocks one has, the higher the chances of getting the insight. The ancient Greek poet Achilochus of Paros said: 'The fox knows many things, but the hedgehog knows one big thing.' In today's VUCA world, better to know many things.

c) Books and newspaper articles are superior tools to provide insight.

The written word demands reflection, the development of a convincing case or plot, the presentation of evidence, verifiable data, a degree of logic, the perspective of time. As such it is very different from some media that thrive on soundbites and emotion. Facebook, Instagram and – all too often – TV just throw ephemeral snippets around. These media are mostly designed to entertain and amuse, not to instruct.

d) Know your classics.

Some dismiss the classical canon as 'dead white males'. How mistaken they are! The classics are classic because successive generations have found inspiration and consolation in them. If earlier stories were - or will be - told from Livy, Arrian, Seneca, and Sun Tzu, it was done with this ulterior motive in mind. I'm in good company: Management guru Peter Drucker recommended Xenophon's (420s–360s BC) *The Persian Expedition* as essential reading. Xenophon was an Athenian who joined a 10,000 strong Greek mercenary army in Persia. They were there to help Prince Cyrus overthrow his brother and seize the throne of the Persian Empire. Eventually the Greeks were betrayed and had to march home through hundreds of miles of hostile terrain. Xenophon was chosen by the men to lead the exit and guide the troops to safety. It remains one of the great practical guides on strategic and operational tactics.[4] Alexander the Great read this book and used it as a guide for his campaigns. Caesar in turn read about Alexander. Caesar's writings in turn inspired Napoleon, an avid collector and reader of books.

In the Strategy course, Yale Professor and Pulitzer Prize winner John Lewis Gaddis rightly insists students read classics such as Tolstoy's *War & Peace*, Machiavelli's *The Prince* (Stalin's favourite by the way) and Clausewitz' *On War*.[5] There is tremendous power in developing analogical thinking capabilities. This is defined as the practice of recognizing conceptual similarities in multiple domains that seem to have little in common on the surface.[6]

To illustrate it, let's review a problem posed by German *Gestalt* psychologist Karl Duncker (1903–40): an oncologist is faced with a tricky problem.[7] One of his patients has a stomach tumor. He cannot operate on the tumor but unless the patient is treated, he is sure to die. There is a ray that can destroy the cancer cells. The trouble is that the ray needs to be delivered with very high intensity. If not, there is no effect. However, a high intensity ray also destroys all the healthy tissue it passes through. No harm is done to healthy tissue at lower intensity levels. So how to solve this dilemma? When people hear two unrelated stories, 30% can solve the problem after the first one, and 80% after the second one.

Story 1: A general was tasked to capture a fortress. If he could concentrate all his troops at the same time, the siege would be successful. There were plenty of roads leading to the fortress, but they were strewn with mines. Only small groups of soldiers could safely move on any road. The general decided to divide his army into small groups. They synchronized their watches and made sure to reach the fortress at the same time despite taking different roads. The plan worked.

Story 2: A small-town fire chief arrived at a fire. Unless it was extinguished quickly, it would spread to neighboring houses. There was no water hydrant but there was a lake nearby. The neighborhood had already formed a line passing buckets. But the single buckets thrown on the fire were not effective. The fire chief ordered a halt to the proceedings. He asked to fill all the buckets at once, to form a circle around the fire and, on the count of three, had the water thrown all at once. The fire was extinguished.

The answer to the radiation problem is to direct low-intensity rays at the tumor from different directions, leaving healthy tissue unharmed, and by convergence around the tumor reach enough intensity to destroy it.

Here's a real-life business example. Can knowledge of pottery of the proto-Mesopotamian period ever prove useful? Yes, by the power of analogical thinking. I had co-designed an office building in Poland. The press booklet for the grand opening was a very expensive arty one. One day before the press event, to my annoyance, I discovered a typo. Artist Roy Lichtenstein's name had been misspelled. But then I remembered a book on Ancient Iraq. The pottery in that period always had a small deliberate blemish, because it was believed that only the gods could reach perfection. I've put a small paper in the booklet telling this story and that therefore this booklet also had its small imperfection. Journalists really liked that touch.

The classics are often fabulously well written, full of incredible adventures. You will discover that people in the past struggled with many of the same questions as us. They dealt with love and heartbreak, victory and defeat, humiliation and glory, envy, ambition, choices, strategy, how to motivate others, how to convince reluctant stakeholders that change is required and how to find allies. There is no adventure as thrilling as the human one. Stories are an essential part of your leadership because they are better remembered than dry prose. It's a great way to pass on knowledge. We are a storytelling species. A story is not the same as information.

Information: 'The king is dead.'

Story: 'The king is dead. He was poisoned by his wife and her secret lover.'

Story with intrigue: 'The king is dead. He was poisoned by his wife and her secret lover. However, they made one crucial mistake. Little did they know that…'

e) You will never be bored again.

A delay of the plane is no issue when you have a great book at hand. If your partner takes more time to get ready for a party, don't get upset! Grab that book or your e-reader and dive into an adventure. The pocketbook has endured because it is light, portable and dirt cheap. For $10 you can get access to some of the best thinking humanity has ever produced. All it takes is for you to read it!

EXECUTIVE SUMMARY:

1. Strategy deployment must always be checked versus the available means and capabilities.
2. It is totally acceptable to identify a strategic 'where to win' area even if one does not yet know how to win, provided a 'Microbattle' plan is designed at lower risk and scale.
3. Competence leads to confidence. It's not the other way around. Competence comes from capabilities.
4. Mastery is a major driver of motivation.
5. One must relentlessly build the capabilities of the organization. The most important resource is human. So, let's build its muscle.
6. You cannot blame people for not knowing what they don't know.
7. Inspiration can come from anywhere, but it must come from somewhere.
8. Personal development is the responsibility of the employee. But the leader must create the conditions into which learning can take place.
9. Leaders should be readers.

D.
NO EXCUSE OWNERSHIP

CHAPTER 10

The Ownership Matrix & The Circle of Influence

The final element of the MSE, and one of the most important, is No Excuse Ownership. Ownership serves as a force multiplier, and without it, all efforts may prove fruitless. It's imperative to instill this mindset throughout the organization, and we will delve into how to achieve this.

One compelling anecdote involves Mr. Robert A. McDonald, former CEO of P&G and former Secretary of Veteran Affairs under President Obama, and his experiences during his initial year at West Point. As a freshman (or 'plebe' in the school's lingo) he was only entitled to three answers when questioned:
- Yes/no.
- I do not understand.
- No excuse.

On the way to a parade, his gray cadet uniform got splashed with mud. He was called out for having failed the standard and was asked why. What's the right response? 'I do not understand?' The only good answer is 'no excuse' (implicit in that answer is of course: 'and it won't happen again').

1. **The leader must consistently demonstrate no excuse ownership.**

The devastating Battle of Gettysburg (July 1–3, 1863) is considered the turning point of the American Civil War. It's the moment when the South lost its offensive capability. What concerns us here is not the ebb and flow of the battle but General Lee's admission after his defeat: 'All this has been my fault – it is I that have lost this fight.'[1] Lee could easily have blamed other causes. There were very significant intelligence failures. Some of his subordinates badly underperformed. But Lee was right. In the end, it was his fault. The leader is responsible for all the elements in the Mission Success Equation. If there is no Strategic Clarity, the leader must fix that. If the Execution is faulty because there are no Capabilities, the leader takes the blame.

2. **Insist on truth and clear language.**

In one company, monthly letters from General Managers sometimes talk about 'negative growth'. Sorry, they made a loss. Insist on calling a spade a spade. Steve Jobs made a point of being honest (admittedly to the point of meanness): 'My job is to say when something sucks rather than sugarcoat it.'[2] His reports found that tough to handle but also admitted that they could never have achieved what they did without that trait. Intel's Andy Grove also had a blunt, no-bullshit style.[3] Even Louis XIV, the very embodiment of the absolutist king who ruled by divine sanction, understood the need for truth.

In 1700, he wrote instructions to his grandson Philippe, the Duke of Anjou. The latter had just been appointed to the throne of Spain as Felipe V. Louis' grandfatherly advice included this tip: 'Beware of flatterers, rely on those who with good intentions dare to contradict you. These are your true friends.'[4] Also, in his own councils, he allowed free debate (though for those present it was wise to keep the Arab proverb in mind: 'the arrow of truth must be dipped in honey').

Get rid of the bullshitters ASAP. In his essay *On Bullshit*, Dr. Frankfurt explains the difference between a liar and bullshitter. The former has a very good notion of the truth but decides to withhold it from you. A bullshitter has no concept of the truth but invents stuff to suit his purpose.[5] Usually, that purpose is 'me, myself and I.' Intellectual honesty is of the utmost importance. The Ancient Greeks had a saying: 'people's speech matches their lives.' The Greek dramatist Aeschylus (525/524 BC–456/455 BC) famously said that 'in war, the first casualty is truth.' That same risk is especially high in a company when there is a crisis, whereas it's the moment when truth has its highest value. Unfortunately, as any student of history knows, it has always been a rather dangerous occupation to be the messenger of bad tidings. We'll discuss how to deal with that issue in the Supercharged Team chapter (Pillar 4).

3. **The leader must be willing to stomach the truth if he or she wants it told.**

I'd add two suggestions:
- Ask to also propose an alternative. It's easy to shoot holes in things but what's needed is constructive criticism that makes the plan better.
- A point can be vigorously advocated but constructive language must be used. Wrongs are often forgiven, contempt never is. We do not tolerate profanity at family dinners, so there's no reason to accept it in a meeting room.

No Excuse Ownership must be made part of the culture. According to Professor Gary P. Pisano from Harvard Business School, while cultures may have pleasant and enjoyable behaviors, they must also be balanced by more rigorous ones.[6] That is a very important statement. Great corporate cultures have both. Said differently, if people want the A-side, they also need to accept a B-side. You can't have one without the other. You want ownership? Great, but it means you are 200% accountable. For example:

A-SIDE	B-SIDE
A tolerance for failure	Intolerance for incompetence
Willingness to experiment	Rigorous discipline
Safe to speak up	Candour & Truth
Ownership	Individual Accountability
Non-hierarchical	Strong leadership

4. Ownership and accountability require a transfer of decision rights.

You cannot expect employees to feel ownership if they have no say in their work decisions. As figure 15 below explains, there is a sweet spot, a balanced position between Decision Rights and Accountability. One without the other leads to issues. Nothing angers as much as to be made accountable for results on which one had no influence at all. Leaders who make the wrong calls but then shove the negative impact off to the lower ranks are universally despised. But to hand out decision rights without the corresponding accountability is irresponsible.

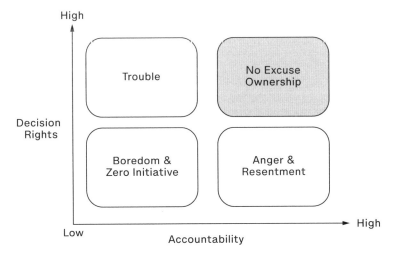

Figure 15: The Accountability Matrix
(Source: based on a discussion with Zest for Leaders Consulting, Brussels)

Figure 16 below shows the ownership matrix.

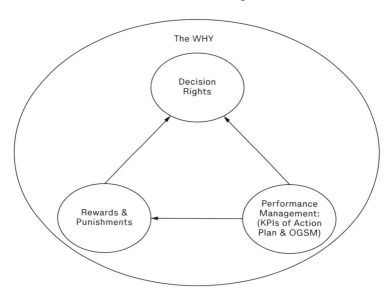

Figure 16: The Ownership Matrix
(Source: based on a seminar run by Monitor for P&G)

As was mentioned earlier, people deliver better if they understand the why, which is the Strategic Clarity provided by the Mission Success Equation, or at lower level by CBAs (see chapter 8). Rewards must be completely in line with what the company wants to achieve. These, in turn, are linked to Decision Rights. The team and employees are evaluated in the areas where they have decision rights. The reward structure is, in turn, based on performance management. The KPIs from the OGSM and the Action Plan (covered in the last chapter) provide the core elements of what needs to be achieved.

5. Increase your circle of influence.

Sometimes I hear: 'I'm only a lowly employee.' It's true that power and position in the hierarchy matter. But it's also a question of mindset. American author Helen Keller was blind and deaf. Yet, she believed: 'I am only one; but I am still one. I cannot do everything, but still I can do something. I will not refuse to do the something I can do.' That's the idea behind Stephen R. Covey's powerful concept of the circles of influence and of concern.[7]

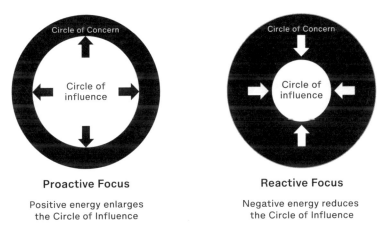

Proactive Focus

Positive energy enlarges the Circle of Influence

Reactive Focus

Negative energy reduces the Circle of Influence

Figure 17: Circle of Concern / Circle of Influence
(© Stephen R. Covey, 'The 7 Habits of Highly Effective People')

As we look at the world around us, there are plenty of things over which we have zero control. We may be concerned about North Korea, but chances are rather slim that our worries or viewpoints will make one iota of difference. We may worry about the weather, hoping it will not rain on our garden party, but we'll have to live with whatever comes our way. As the Stoic Seneca wisely taught: 'That which we cannot reform, it is best to endure.' All these things belong in the circle of concern. There are however lots of activities that we can influence. We can decide to come with a smile into the office on Monday morning. We can be fitter, be more helpful to others, arrive on time in meetings, treat people with respect and dignity. Surprisingly, none of these activities require a Harvard degree nor an investment budget. The more we pro-actively manage our circle of influence, the greater our influence becomes.

> **EXECUTIVE SUMMARY:**
>
> 1. Ownership is a force multiplier. If it is zero, everything becomes naught. It's a mindset, an attitude.
> 2. The leader must demonstrate extreme ownership.
> 3. Insist on truth and clear language.
> 4. The leader must be willing to stomach the truth if he or she wants it told.
> 5. Ownership and accountability require a transfer of decision rights.
> 6. Increase your circle of influence.

E.
A HARD-WON IRON MAN VICTORY TO SUMMARIZE THE MISSION SUCCESS EQUATION

Early 2002, Marc Herremans' dream to win the Iron Man seemed over. 'Worse,' Marc thought, 'my life is over,' as he lay completely paralyzed on the rocky soil. Until that moment, his life had been bliss. As an exceptionally gifted athlete, Marc had raked in success after success. He had also served his country in Belgium's elite para-commando regiment. Everybody knew for certain that one day he'd win the world's toughest triathlon. He participated for the first time in 2001 and had come in sixth. His whole life revolved around one mission: winning that race. It was to prepare for another season that he was training in Lanzarote. On that fateful January 28, 2002, Marc went for a routine bike ride. At some point, a car was in the way. As he swerved to avoid it, his front wheel slid off the road. He took a tumbling fall. 99% of the time, one walks away with bruises, a good dinner anecdote or at worst a broken bone or two. Marc landed his spine on a sharp stone. It snapped.

By the time he was in hospital, Herremans regained the use of his arms. For a moment there was a faint flicker of hope. But the doctor's final verdict left no room for doubt. He would forever be paralyzed from the diaphragm down. Now what?

Renewed Strategic Clarity: understandably, Marc went through a depression. But then, he had an enlightening thought: the mission was not over. He could still win the Iron Man, in the race for disabled athletes. Herremans took up training again. A win would be hard because, contrary to what happens in the Paralympics, there is only one category for disabled athletes. Some were 'only' paralyzed from the waist down. They still had the use of their abdominal muscles. Also, the timing when one became disabled plays a role. It may sound heartless but those who had a limitation since childhood had an advantage since their muscles had been trained to the new condition earlier.

Capabilities: everything was now to be done via arm strength. In swimming, paralyzed legs are splinted so that they remain straight in the water. Cycling is done via a hand bike, the marathon via a wheelchair. Marc had never used any of those. He now needed a two-man team to carry him out of the water towards the hand bike. New training methods and race strategies were needed.

No Excuse Ownership: he was back in Hawaii in 2002. Amazingly, this was only ten months after his accident. He confessed that the hardest part was mindset. From being independent, he was now often dependent on others. He always loved running and cycling. Whilst the mission was as much alive as before, he now had to train things he liked but little. He was often sick as a by-product of his accident. Marc said: 'What drove me on was this belief that I broke my back, but not my dreams. I had the feeling that my accident was a grave injustice, that something essential had been taken away from me, I refused to let that happen.'

Perfect Execution: after unsuccessful attempts, he finally won the 2006 Iron Man. A race typically took 10 to 11 hours of blood, sweat and tears. The interesting thing is that he now looks back at the accident with a different perspective. He calls it 'a U-Turn'. 'I used to be very self-centred, maybe one needs to be selfish to compete at the very top, but now my focus is on helping others.' Herremans started the *To Walk Again* foundation* and he's the driving force behind *Athletes for Hope* in Belgium. Amongst others, these charities provide disabled children with opportunities to do sports. It is touching to see even completely paralyzed children participate with joy. How? Via a tube in their mouth, they blow a ping pong ball at each other. Or they put a ball under their chin and let it roll down a slope in a game called bochia. These children helped Marc win his Iron Man. Having reviewed footage of the race, I noticed that Marc suffered terribly at several points. I asked what gave him the required resilience. He provided a deep response: 'People tend to look up. This woman makes more money than me. She is so much more beautiful than I am. This guy drives a car I'll never be able to afford. But we must also learn to look down. When I felt that I could not go on, I contemplated those kids. What would they not give to be able to use their arms? I thought:

* www.towalkagain.be

'You are in Hawaii pursuing your dream. Don't you even think of giving up.'

In the *Born on the Fourth of July* biopic, there is one deeply moving scene that sticks forever in my mind. After being badly wounded in Vietnam, US Marine Ron Kovic (Tom Cruise) is wheelchair bound. He's in despair and asks his mother: 'Who's going to love me now?' Marc's experience is similar. 'When I visit those in hospital who had similar accidents as mine, they do not worry about flashy things. They worry about being loved. They wonder if they can still have a family.' One could say that giving hope is his new mission. As Navy SEAL Rob Robertson (ret.) convincingly claims: 'Hope is the strength faith needs to prevail. One does not exist without the other.'[1]

Marc's experience demonstrates that we can redefine ourselves. Mr. Ron Kovic also found new purpose in his opposition to the Vietnam war. At the very least, their stories illustrate two other key pillars: disruptions happen, it's a VUCA world and we may be confronted with the need for change. Marc also claimed he'd walk again, because one day there will be a scientific breakthrough. And he does. Marc runs, dances, and jumps in the shape of his son and two daughters.

This story concludes the first part of the book. Every element has been reviewed of the Mission Success Equation. One could compare it to a walk in the forest. Strategic Clarity is the compass. Capabilities provide the kit, the skills to read a map and to do an azimuth. Perfect Execution means not drifting into a swamp and arriving at the destination. It's up to you to get there.

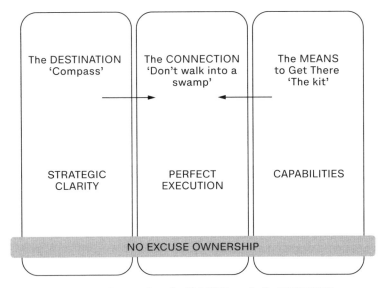

Figure 18: The Mission Success Equation (© 2019 Peter Corijn / VUCASTAR)

In the next part, we will review the F.A.Y.U.R. methodology.

EXECUTIVE SUMMARY:

1. The Mission Success Equation ('MSE')
   = (Strategic Clarity + Capabilities
   + Perfect Execution) x No Excuse Ownership.

PILLAR 2

F.A.Y.U.R.
Fluid Strategy and Execution
Agility
Your leadership
Understanding
Resilience

In the following five chapters we will discuss each element of F.A.Y.U.R., starting with Napoleon's greatest misadventure, from which we will draw important business lessons.

FLUID STRATEGY AND EXECUTION

THE RUSSIAN WINTER

Inhabitants of Vilnius in Lithuania were surprised when on December 9, 1812, the remnants of Napoleon's Grande Armée drifted back into town. They were dirty, starving, sick, full of lice, and covered in all sorts of clothes as protection against the brutal Russian winter. Some wore liturgical vestments; others wore ladies' dresses over their threadbare uniforms. Any piece of textile was welcome to add another layer of warmth. These troops resembled nothing like the proud regiments that had departed just six months earlier to defeat Russia. Of the 600,000 strong invasion army – at that time the biggest the world had ever seen – as many as 400,000 had perished. A further 100,000 were captured. Most would not survive the brutal captivity conditions for long. 160,000 horses died. A thousand cannon were lost. It was a defeat of epic proportions.

The reason for going to war was that Napoleon had fallen out with his erstwhile ally, Tsar Alexander I, over the implementation of the Continental System. This was a blockade designed to destroy British commerce and consequently the ability of the British government to continue the fight against France. The Russians had agreed to implement the system after the treaties of Tilsit (1807) and Erfurt (1808). They had little choice after a painful trouncing by Napoleon at the battles of Austerlitz and Friedland. However, by 1810, the relationship between the two nations had soured. The fact was that the Continental System was crippling the Russian economy. On top, as ever, there was a burning desire for revenge after the earlier defeats. This explosive cocktail of economic hardship and hurt pride made it impossible for Tsar Alexander to continue the status quo.

Napoleon saw this as a *casus belli*. His army crossed the river Niemen into Russia on June 24, 1812. Interestingly, the Russian army was positioned right at the border. Bonaparte's plan was a quick and decisive victory in that area. That had always been his tactic: move fast, leave the enemy no time to prepare, concentrate large forces at the right point before the enemy had time to understand what was going on, deliver a decisive blow and then dictate terms. The emperor was not planning to be dragged deep into Russia. Speed was also needed for logistical reasons. Even for a short 50-day campaign the numbers required were staggering: 600,000 men require 30 million rations of bread and rice and three million bushels of oats to feed horses. 28 million bottles of wine and two million of brandy were carried.

The Russians were only too aware of Bonaparte's strategy and had no intention to offer battle to Napoleon's superior numbers and command. Mikhail Barclay de Tolly, war minister and in charge of the Russian army, kept retreating. That way the French would be increasingly stretched from a logistics point of view. It was not a popular strategy in the Russian army. It was hard for the troops to see their country devastated without offering a fight. Soon, there were more and more rumours of treason by the 'German' (Barclay was of Baltic German descent). The Tsar was pressured to replace Barclay with the elderly Russian Mikhail Kutuzov who promptly continued the retreat, ever deeper into the heartland. Napoleon followed in the forlorn hope that he'd be able to deliver a decisive blow or that the Tsar would be forced to negotiate.

Every time, the French Emperor convinced himself that the Russians would halt and fight. He was sure they'd not give up Smolensk and certainly not Moscow. But they did after the inconclusive battle of Borodino. They even burned Moscow down when the French army entered. In the end, Napoleon had no choice but to turn back and leave. He left too late in the season and was caught in the Russian winter, which proved fatal for his army. The retreat quickly turned into unmitigated horror. On March 31, 1814, the Russian Tsar victoriously entered Paris. Bonaparte was forced into his first exile.

1. **The core business lesson here is that competition also has a vote.**

They know your strengths and weaknesses and will adjust their strategy accordingly. Napoleon had gotten used to surprising his adversaries and to control events. Now that somebody else did it to him he was bewildered and lost. These people were just not acting as they ought to. From the first contact in the Russian campaign, it was clear that this was a different type of war. It was total war. The Russians burned everything before their retreat, the population fled, and little to nothing was left for the invaders. Russia was mostly dirt poor, sparsely populated with subsistence farmers who could only just avoid starvation during normal times. There was close to no food to be obtained. The roads were a disaster, full of clouds of dust in the heat of summer but near impassable quagmires as soon as it rained. Progress was slow. Tens of thousands of men died of disease, hunger and thirst on the march. On hot days, soldiers would throw themselves on the ruts in the road filled with horse urine to get something to drink. There was only empty, barren space.

Russian soldiers also fought differently. They fought until death and never surrendered (as other armies did), in turn leading to higher casualty rates amongst the French. Russians were used to battling the Turks. In these engagements, quarter was never received, nor given.[1] ***One cannot but recall Prussian Field Marshall von Moltke's (1800–1891) wise dictum that no plan survives contact.*** He saw strategy as 'a system of expedients'. World Heavyweight Boxing Champion (1987–90) Mike Tyson put the same concept more prosaically as: 'Everybody has a plan until they get punched in the face.' ***In net, mission success requires strategic and executional fluidity.*** How?

2. **Practice contingency planning: have a plan B. Consider 'What Ifs' before implementing a plan or strategy.**

There is power in positive thinking, but also in complementary negative thinking. They are the yin and yang of good strategic planning. It's useful to have a couple of alternatives ready, 'What Ifs', in case things do not go as initially planned. That way one does not panic or freeze when the proverbial trouble hits the fan. (Ret.) Navy SEAL David Havens says: 'The reality is this – if it walks like a duck, and talks like a duck, have a plan in case it is a chicken.'[2]

It's not as easy as it looks because of the optimism trap. All too often those expressing a desire for a fall-back plan are accused of being negative, pessimists, defeatists. They just do not 'believe' in the company (in Pillar 4, we'll discuss some survival tips for those daring to speak up). Unbounded optimism is a much greater danger. In my experience, 'confident realism', or 'rational optimism' is best. This is also expressed in the 'Stockdale Paradox', named after Admiral Jim Stockdale. He spent eight years in the 'Hanoi Hilton' prisoner of war camp during the Vietnam War. He was tortured over 20 times but survived. Jim Collins interviewed the admiral for his seminal *Good to Great* book. He asked: 'Who did not make it?'

Stockdale claimed the optimists did not make it. This answer surprised Mr. Collins and he asked for clarification. 'The optimists. Oh, they were the ones who said: "We're going to be out by Christmas." And Christmas would come, and Christmas would go. Each time the optimists set their hope on a date, it would pass, and the release would not happen. And they died of a broken heart.'

The paradox lies in the fact that one must at the same time retain faith that one will prevail in the end despite difficulties yet confront the most brutal facts of reality.[3] An executive from a French multinational asked a very interesting question: 'How many "what ifs" does one need? And how do I avoid that this leads to endless discussions because we French love

nothing better than to philosophize?' This gets managed by setting the following rules:
a. 'What If' prediction must lead to preparation. If not, it is just intellectualizing.
b. Only predictions that pass the RICE test, are prepared for.
   Reliability: is there a high possibility and probability?
   Importance of impact of the What If.
   Cost of the preparation.
   Effectiveness of the preparation.[4]
c. Limit the What Ifs to three.

What Ifs may take up resources. So does fire insurance. If one never has an issue, a lot of money was paid for nothing. But then we just never know.

3. Have a reserve and create resource agility.

Julius Caesar, despite being a strategic genius, was always cautious and prepared for unforeseen circumstances. He consistently held back reserves and built a camp at his rear, ready to retreat to in case the battle did not go as planned.

At the battle of Borodino (September 7, 1812), 120 km from Moscow, Napoleon held back his elite Imperial Guard. His Marshals pleaded to release them during the day. However, he refused. Bonaparte knew full well that the war was not over. Being 2,800 km away from his base in Paris, troops could not easily be replaced and certainly not elite troops. The rest of the campaign proved he was probably right in this. The Russians avoided a direct confrontation during Napoleon's retreat as they still feared the fighting skills of this particular corps. His counterpart, the Russian Marshall Kutuzov gets a lot of bad press ('lazy, old, demented, stupid') but the old fox was shrewder than many give him credit for. He preferred to give Napoleon the illusion of a way out during the retreat. He had not read Sun Tzu* but that Chinese general would very much have agreed. Kutuzov told his staff that if cornered, the French would fight to the end and even a victory would be very costly. Better to let the Russian winter do its part and destroy stragglers piecemeal.

Resource agility is hard to achieve. Several executives will fight tooth and nail to keep their budgets and their best people, even if they will pay lip service to Agility. Of course, the CEO can always make a hard call. Here are three simple ways to get it without too much trouble:

a. Insist on an 'unearmarked' portion as part of the yearly budget process, say 5% or 10%. It can only be released upon agreement by the CEO. It can also be taken away from a given division and be injected somewhere else. It's easier to take away an 'unearmarked' part of a budget because a given division in a way never owned it in the first place.

b. Set a general rule of a 48/52 spending split for both halves of the year (unless there is major seasonality). If not, and everything is spent upfront when a crisis hits, there is nothing left to recover.

c. Establish a fair process upfront to alter the objectives (including for the sacred bonus) should significant resources be taken away from a given division.

---

* Sun Tzu: 'To a surrounded enemy you must leave a way of escape.' 'Do not press an enemy at bay.'

4. Dare to retreat and to change course.

It's hard on the ego and therefore rather unpopular. Failure, perceived or otherwise, carries a stigma. It will indeed be immediately exploited by competitors inside and outside the company. Napoleon was very much influenced by how an early Russian retreat would look in the eyes of other nations. It would certainly have been bad PR. However, it would have saved his army and most probably his throne. I'm not arguing to give up easily. But sometimes the writing is on the wall, and one does better to change course. The sober Dutch have another great proverb: 'Beter ten halve gekeerd dan ten hele verkeerd.' Better to turn around halfway than to be completely wrong.

Humans suffer from the 'sunk cost fallacy'. Once we have invested time, money, and effort into something, it is increasingly hard to walk away from it. It's well documented that we feel a potential loss much more keenly than a potential gain. Perhaps this is a good place to discuss how to deal with failure. All too often, when things go awry, the first question is 'who's wrong?' rather than 'what's wrong?' Little wonder then that employees hide bad news or excel in putting a positive spin on things. This does not mean that identifying the 'who' is without merit. Those in charge must be held accountable. Leadership makes a difference. It's just that only asking the whodunnit question does not lead to sufficient in-depth understanding. It creates the wrong culture.

5. **Failure only has worth if it generates learning and does so at an acceptable cost.**

A mess created by sheer stupidity has little value. Also, it's not very useful if obtained at the price of bankruptcy. Bonaparte learned quite a bit from his misadventure in Russia in 1812. Alas, his army was destroyed. *Issues can be attributed to three core areas: failure*
a. to anticipate the future;
b. to learn from the past;
c. to adapt to the present.[5]

When all three are in play, disaster follows. Napoleon did not anticipate the harshness of the Russian winter and underestimated the strategic depth of the country. For a long time, he joked that the weather in Fontainebleau in France (where his castle was) was worse than in Russia. He did not learn from the past either. Earlier, the Swedish king Charles XII had ended up badly in Russia against Peter the Great (at Poltava). Napoleon was an avid reader and connoisseur of books. He had read Voltaire's *History of Charles XII* and Gustavus Alderfeld's account of the doomed Swedish expedition. The risks of the Russian winter and the dogged resilience of the Russians were highlighted in there, but to no avail. There was a lack of adaptation. As winter approached, allied Polish cavalry officers started to put special horseshoes on their mounts to provide stability on icy ground. That practice was dismissed as a quirk. Precious food was substituted for loot in the baggage train during the retreat.

The following tools are available:

a. Anticipating the future:
   i. *Report Near Misses*: those are usually covered up with a sigh of relief. But a near miss indicates a major weakness where an issue was averted by the smallest of margins or by dumb luck. It's an accident waiting to happen. Create a culture where they are reported and acted upon.
   ii. *Pre-Mortem*. Here one asks the question *before* an initiative as follows: 'Imagine we failed, why would that have happened?' Perhaps because the competitive reaction was underestimated. The plan is then re-evaluated against these concerns.
   iii. A crucially important point: if you are always the devil's advocate, you'll be sidelined quickly as 'a negative person', whether you are right or not. Therefore, *make challenge part of the process*, not any individual's role (see the Supercharged Team section, Pillar 4).
   iv. *Constantly have a roster of small tests – ongoing - to evaluate possible future options*. It's certainly better to put a small learning test out there versus an endless yes/no debate in the office.

b. Learning from the past:
   i. *As already covered, have candid after-action reviews.* Make it part of the process. Ensure that not only the good is mentioned but also what could have been done better. Capture the learnings and make sure to communicate them broadly to the organization, if only to avoid similar mistakes in the future.

ii. *Run 'what's hot, what's not' sessions* where each executive needs to highlight one positive learning and one based on failure.

c. Adapting to the present.
LEAN is usually associated with a manufacturing process. But the principles are just as valid in other business areas. Suffice to name three:
   i. *Go and See.* Nothing beats first-hand experience. In-homes, storechecks, meetings with customers and employees.
   ii. *Respect the frontline.* Those who are in touch with the reality of the marketplace deserve respect. Their experience and ideas are very valuable. Hence, give enough freedom to those employees. In some categories (like laundry detergents), it is a 'game of inches'. Local ideas and tactics can make a decisive difference. The additional benefit is that it provides autonomy to employees and a sense of being in charge of one's own destiny.
   iii. *Always challenge.* Never be complacent. There is always a better way. One option: let outsiders do the challenge. For instance, use an outside agency to penetrate your security. Ex-Special Forces were asked to get into our office building without raising any alarm. The next morning, we found a little 'hi' note on our desks. Some would dumpster dive and come up with confidential documents. This effort allowed us to close gaps in security.

I'd like to state that a constant 100% success rate indicates a problem too. It means no risk was ever taken.

6. Tactical capability makes a critical difference once engaged.

≡ Tactics are part of execution excellence. Recall: these are planned and ad hoc activities, meant to deal with the demands of the moment and to move from one milestone to another in pursuit of the overall strategic goal(s).

There are five key factors to consider as per figure 19.

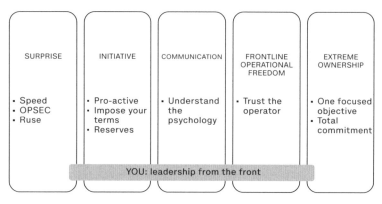

Figure 19: Tactics – Critical Factors (© 2018 Peter Corijn / VUCASTAR)

a. Surprise is always great:

> Absolutely avoid being predictable. For years, at P&G Morocco, the last quarter spending was always cut to make up for profit shortfalls. So, when would you launch your initiative against P&G? Competitors aren't stupid and will exploit that tactical advantage.

OPSEC ('Operations Security') is important in this respect. P&G used to be rightly paranoid about it. When P&G's

Always entry into Feminine protection in Belgium was planned, it was given a codename ('Delta'). The team was located on a different floor, out of bounds for everybody else. Best to use code names for important initiatives. Practice a 'need to know' policy. Yes, it is acceptable to tell some employees that they should not be in the know. People love to talk and to show off, that's the danger. Check that documents are not left lying on desks or on the copy machine after close of business. Set clear rules in this respect.

Do use deception (of course legally). Here's a true story. For NDA reasons, I use codewords. Competitor 'Alpha' had a critical business in Category 1 and played in Category 2. For the other company, 'Beta', Category 2 was vital. Beta was also active in Category 1, but their brand was a total dog.

COMPANY	ALPHA	BETA
Category 1	Vital, core business	Weak, non-core
Category 2	Important	Vital, core business

Beta cut the price of their weak Category 1 brand to rock bottom, by -30%. Not because they had any interest in developing the brand. They suspected that Alpha would see it as an existential threat, defend their position vigorously and throw serious money at it. But Beta had all along planned an all-important Category 2 initiative three months after the Category 1 price cut. When the Category 2 initiative hit, Alpha could not defend well because they had spent so much budget on shoring up Category 1. Beta scored a major success in their core business.

Now that would have made the master, Sun Tzu, proud. Be a lion but don't forget to be a cunning fox as well.

b. Be pro-active and impose your terms:

In May 1940, the Germans overwhelmed the French and English armies completely. They had a great new tactic called *Blitzkrieg* ('lightning war'). This novel military tactic was designed to create psychological shock and havoc in enemy forces through the deployment of surprise and speed. Panzer troops created a breach in enemy lines, supported by 'Stuka' dive bombers, and would relentlessly rush forward. The less mobile infantry only followed later to mop things up. The big advantage of such a tactic is that it constantly imposes terms on competitors. It's always better to be proactive and control the situation rather than having to respond to it. The concept was already highlighted when game changers were discussed in chapter 4.

c. Communication – understand the psychology:

The 77-year-old Marshall Kutuzov is usually denigrated in accounts of the 1812 Russian campaign against Napoleon Bonaparte. Admittedly, Kutuzov was no strategic genius. Yet, he had one big advantage over all his contenders: he understood the Russian soul. He knew that the Russian soldier fought best and doggedly in defensive positions. Hence, he positioned his troops to take full advantage of that quality at the Battle of Borodino. On that fateful morning of September 6, 1812, he did not give a rousing speech to the troops. To the amusement of the observing French army, he asked all soldiers to kneel for a procession of singing monks waving frankincense. They carried the icon of the Black Virgin of Smolensk with them. Kutuzov understood the mystic yearning of the average Russian soldier (a brutally treated and uneducated serf who was enlisted for 25 years and, some exceptions notwithstanding, could never hope to see his village again). His men fought literally to the death and denied the French the decisive victory they so badly needed. It would take the Somme battle in WWI to break the sad record of the casualty list. It's that sort of understanding, that kind of communication that can provide a tactical advantage, the extra courage needed to help a team to hold on.

d. Frontline operational freedom:

Employees who have contact with the marketplace must have decision rights to be able to act fast and decisively. ***There is, however, one important prerequisite: there must be unity of doctrine***. If not, one gets chaos. That brings us back to the need for strategic clarity from the Mission Success Equation; discussed at length. Go-to-Market Models and CBAs also provide crucial guidance. It's important not only to allow operational freedom but also to train the capability of the organization in this respect.

e. No Excuse Ownership, total commitment:

Here it pops up again. It's indeed the vital ingredient. However, no need to repeat the concept (see Pillar 1, chapter 10).

f. Leadership from the front:

We'll cover that in the 'Y' of F.A.Y.U.R. (Pillar 2, 3).

EXECUTIVE SUMMARY:

1. Competition has a vote, and no plan survives contact.
2. Hence, develop contingency plans, upfront.
3. Keeping reserves is essential unless the situation gets desperate.
4. Dare to retreat and change course.
5. Failure can be a great source of learning.
6. Tactics can provide a major advantage once engaged. Drive decision rights down in the organization but equally ensure unity of doctrine.

AGILITY
JESTERS ARE NO FOOLS

≡ Agility: the ability to swiftly innovate and/or to react with discipline to change or emerging opportunities to stay competitive and to win.

As a warm-up, here are three examples of superb thinking agility. Consider how you'd get out of the situation. What jesters said and did is on the next page.

i. Akbar the Great (1542–1605) was the third Mughal emperor in India. Akbar had a parrot he loved more than any of his other pets. He warned his servants that they must look after it well. The emperor added that whoever brought him the news of the parrot's death would be killed. Alas, despite excellent care, the parrot did die. Not surprisingly, everybody was afraid to tell Akbar. His jester Birbal came up with an approach. What's yours?

ii. Henri II (1519–1559) was King of France and entertaining at his Fontainebleau chateau. Amidst the merrymakers, his jester was cracking jokes. The fool then made a major faux pas. He made a pun about the Queen's dress that fell completely flat. The King erupted in anger and condemned his fool to death. But he added: 'Because I'm merciful, I'll let you choose the way you'll die.' So, how do you want to die? What's your answer?

iii. Notker the Stammerer, a monk who wrote a ninth century biography of Charlemagne, had this story to share:

Charlemagne's ambassador was invited to a dinner with the Byzantine Emperor in what is now Istanbul. At that court, they had a rule that no guest at the emperor's table should turn over any animal or part of any animal served on a dish. One must only eat the upper part. Alas, the envoy was not aware of the custom. When a fish was placed before him, he promptly turned the fish over. The other nobles present rose in indignation and cried: 'Master, you are dishonored, as none of your ancestors ever was before you!' The emperor was troubled and said to the envoy: 'I cannot resist them: you must be put to death at once.' His Majesty however added that the envoy could make one last wish, except to spare his life. Any other request would be granted. How to get out of this scrape alive?

i. The dead parrot:

Birbal went to tell Akbar in great excitement how wonderful the bird was. It had turned into a yogi in a state of samadhi (a state of profound and absorptive contemplation). The emperor wanted to see this miracle right away only to find the parrot dead.
He shouted enraged: 'The bird isn't in samadhi, you fool! He's dead!'
The jester replied: 'Your Highness must die, according to your own decree, for telling you that the parrot is dead.'
Akbar had no choice but to admit his own folly and forgave all.[1]

ii. How do you want to die?

The buffoon answered: 'Of old age, Sire.'
The King was amused by the answer and asked: 'And when is that?'
'The day just before your own death, Sire.'
The jester was forgiven on the spot.[2]

iii. The ambassador:

He asked the emperor: 'With my dying breath, I ask one favour; let everyone who saw me turn over that fish be deprived of his eyes.'

The emperor promptly swore that he had seen nothing of the kind. He had only trusted the word of others. Then the queen excused herself. She hadn't noticed anything. The nobles followed her example. The ambassador went home safe and sound.[3]

What is the agile equivalent for a business? A good starting point is figure 20 on the following page. It's important to decide where you stand on the different components and to consider the potential trade-offs. More speed may be needed but it might entail more risk or have an impact on quality.

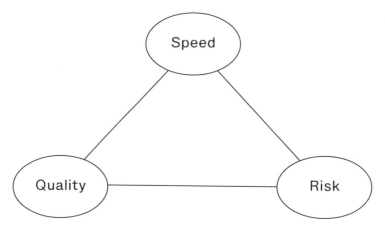

Figure 20: The Agility Triangle
(Source: model used by Product Supply at Imperial Brands)

Some questions to ask:
(i) In which parts of the business do we need agility and where not?
(ii) Then, can we have agility in the chosen area? Can we manage the risk and quality impact? The concept of Minimum Viable Products (MVPs) is prevalent in Silicon Valley. However, it's not feasible to launch an MVP in the baby food industry as the consequences of failure can be dire. For instance, if two babies were to fall seriously ill, it could destroy the brand's reputation. The aviation industry operates under similar constraints. Nobody wants to go aboard an MVP plane to help engineers figure out design flaws. Sure, the black box will provide insights when the craft crashes, but I'd rather not be on it.

Upfront, let me state that the methodology for agile innovation will not be discussed in these pages. It's a topic that requires its own book.[4] Rather, three concepts will be shared that will have an important impact on the nimbleness of your business.

1. Trust builds speed (and reduces cost).

Imagine that you have just won the New York Lotto. Two banks, from two different countries, are calling to manage the money for you. One bank is from Switzerland, the other from Pakistan. You must choose one of the two. Which bank do you pick? I'm 99% sure you've decided to go with the Swiss. Maybe that is unfair. Perhaps the Pakistanis are absolute whizz kids. Under which conditions would you go with the Pakistani offer? If you could get the support of lawyers and if the reward was much higher versus the Swiss offer to offset the political risk. All of that would take time and money. That's the difference trust makes. Trust is not some soft hippy dippy concept but a hard economic one. Trust must be built on several levels.[5]

a) It all starts with us as individuals and the credibility required to be believable as a leader. Stephen M.R. Covey distinguishes four elements in this respect:[6]
   i. *Integrity*: do as you say and say as you do. Nothing kills trust faster than hypocrisy.
   ii. *Intent:* what's the agenda and motivation behind your actions? Do you genuinely care or is self-promotion at the heart of your behavior?
   iii. *Capabilities:* I'm sure you trust your partner. But when you need an open-heart operation, you'd probably rather have it done by a surgeon with the right qualifications and capabilities.
   iv. *Results:* we trust leaders who deliver.

b) In relationships, consistent behavior builds trust. Incidentally, the trick dictators use is to change the rules all the time. They of course do not strive for trust but for fear and confusion.

c) At an organizational level, alignment around the Mission Success Equation is vital.

d) In the market and society, reputation matters.

I've asked Navy SEALs if they all like each other. 'Hell no,' came the answer, 'but we trust each other. We know every other man is qualified and will lay down his life for his buddies and country.' That's the spirit one wants in the organization.

2. Develop Learning Agility

Following a speech by Thomas Friedman covering his book *The World is Flat*, a great question was raised: 'If my kids are now competing with boys and girls from Bangalore, São Paolo, and Cape Town in a flat global world, what advice should I give them?'

Mr. Friedman answered: 'learn how to learn'. It makes sense because in a VUCA world, today's knowledge and experience may not be worth much a couple of years down the road.

Executive search firms use learning agility as a key criterion to evaluate candidates. Head-hunter Philiep Dedrijvere explained that performance is quite easy to assess: share and profit are up or down. What's harder to gauge is potential.

He said: 'Learning agility is the lead indicator for high potential. It's knowing what to do when you do not know.'[7] Mr. Dedrijvere provided five dimensions.

i. *Self-awareness*: is there a constant look-out for feedback? Is the way the executive sees him- or herself in line with the opinion of others?
ii. *Agility towards others*: the ability to walk in the shoes of others, to bring the best out of a team.
iii. *Change agility*: can this executive lead transformation efforts? (Pillar 3).
iv. *Results agility*: the capability to deliver, even when the going gets tough.
v. *Mental agility*: is the leader curious, able to make new connections, embracing complexity?

3. Simplify, simplify, simplify.

There are many reasons why Nazi Germany lost the war against the Soviet Union. What may surprise you is that the USSR was better at a capitalist invention: mass production. They outperformed the German economy with a less skilled workforce and less resources. One of the Soviet advantages was extreme simplification. There were two main tanks (the legendary T-34 and the KV-1) and five main aircraft types. At some point in the war, Germany was producing no less than 425 different aircraft models and variations. By the middle of the war, they employed 151 makes of lorry, and 150 different motorcycles.[8] Too many SKUs (Stock-Keeping Units) are a drag on agility. Therefore, install an annual 'kill or cure' exercise. Variants not making a minimum standard must be removed. Also, implement the rule of 'one SKU in, one SKU out'. Or, as FMCG giant Unilever did, 'one SKU in = 2 SKUs out'. Move to power SKUs, the items where the bulk of the sales are.

Most businesses' revenue and profit are usually focused on a couple of brands and markets, which provides scope for simplification. That certainly was the case at P&G. The core business was in roughly 65 labels competing in ten product categories. It was wisely decided to sell off more than 100 non-core brands, as of 2014. There are many reasons for the stock rally of the past years but the fact remains that since that slimming exercise the company performed outstandingly well ($85 in September 2014, $150 April 2023).

Interestingly, at P&G, when we reduced the number of SKUs in store in some categories, consumers reported that they now had more choice. Before, the number of SKUs was simply overwhelming. It all became a blur in a case of seeing a forest, but not recognizing individual trees (just stand in front of the breakfast cereal shelf to see what I mean). I'm sure you've played the children's game of 'telephone' at some point. It's remarkable how fast a message gets distorted when passed along in a chain of seven or fewer people. It happens in your company as well. There are two ways to tackle this:

a. ***Increase spans and reduce management layers.*** This saves cost but the real advantage is in greater speed in decision-making and communication. Also, if people have more span, they become too busy for micromanagement. This in turn empowers the organization and the frontline. Autonomy is a key driver of employee satisfaction.

b. ***Insist on simple and concise writing.*** During WWII, Prime Minister Winston Churchill was fed up with the masses of paper that ended up in his 'black box' every day. Amid a rising tide of urgent war matters, he penned a minute to all Cabinet members, appropriately called *Brevity*. His frustration will sound familiar to most business executives: 'To do our work, we all have to read a mass of papers. Nearly all of them are far too long. This wastes time, while energy has to be spent looking for the essential points.' He then went on to give clear instructions on how notes should be written.[9] Churchill subsequently refused to read anything that was longer than one page. P&G used to have the ironclad rule of the one-page memo as well. Anybody joining the company had to learn the company's writing style. Rather, one had to unlearn a lot of things. In school we had been encouraged to use synonyms, poetic metaphors, and the occasional *pars pro toto* in our essays. All that had to go. First choice words and a simple structure were required. It was a sort of bootcamp. I rewrote my first Nielsen share summary 13 times. But the one-page memo proved an incredibly powerful communication tool. If only because – as Churchill noted – 'the discipline of setting out the real points concisely will prove an aid to clear thinking.'

Mr. Paul Polman underscored that 'agility is not equal to mere restructuring'. It may involve restructuring but it's about having an holistic plan, including all the points made above. Unilever launched 'project half': 'half the time, half the people, half the cost, double the speed'.[10]

4. Agility still requires bureaucracy, albeit a streamlined one.

Books on Ancient China or Byzantium often decry the heavy bureaucracy. But what nobody ever explains is how to run Ancient China or Byzantium without bureaucracy. Equally, large organizations need a degree of it. Of course, it's a good idea to make the processes as light as possible but key things will still need to be reported, both inside and outside the company.

Proper documentation also protects you. Consider this discussion:

Plant Manager: 'Hi, we still have these 100,000 promotion premiums you've ordered. What do you want to do with them?'
Brand Manager: 'Premiums?'
Plant Manager: 'Yes, you ordered them last March.'
Brand Manager: 'No, we said we were considering it.'
Plant Manager: 'No way, you must pay for them.'
Brand Manager: 'Not at all.'

A signed document is then an amazing memory recovery tool. In my experience, when things go well, bureaucracy feels like a drag. But when things go wrong, it can be a lifesaver.

EXECUTIVE SUMMARY:

1. Trust builds speed and reduces cost.
2. Learning Agility is critical.
3. Simplify, simplify, simplify.
4. Agility still requires bureaucracy, albeit a streamlined one.

YOUR LEADERSHIP
THE HARDER RIGHT

The Dutch rationalist philosopher Baruch Spinoza (1632–1677) argued that the question was not whether the ruler was good or bad. The question was to organize the state in such a way that it would not matter whether the ruler was good or bad. In a way, that's what this book tries to achieve. It provides a process and tools. Putting the right processes in place is also important to ensure sustainability. Leaders come and go. Some resign, some get thrown out, some move to new jobs, but the show must go on. Yet, the leader makes a massive difference too. It's up to you to make the mission succeed. Hence, a couple of thoughts in this respect.

1. Choose the harder right versus the easier wrong.

This is a very inspirational phrase from the Cadet's Prayer on display in the West Point Chapel: 'Make us to choose the harder right instead of the easier wrong, and never to be content with a half truth when the whole can be won.' Here's an example. Upon becoming CEO of Unilever, Paul Polman took the courageous decision to no longer provide quarterly reporting or guidance. The company would focus on long-term value, including very ambitious ESG and sustainability goals. That wasn't popular but it was the right thing to do. Across Mr. Polman's tenure, shareholder return was 300%.

I also got this wonderful leadership advice from a rabbi. He told me: 'Imagine the world is exactly 50 percent good and 50 percent bad. Your actions as an individual will make the scale move to the good or the bad side.'

2. Practice leadership from the front.

General Moshe Dayan (1915–1981) was once asked the reason for the prowess of Israeli arms. He answered that it was because officers never ordered soldiers 'forward' but shouted 'follow me'. Commando officer Denis Christiaens added: 'Never ask to do anything that you would not do yourself. Prove it'.[1]

> When the time came at P&G Morocco to announce the painful restructuring, I went to the plants to give the bad news to workers. I could have delegated it because in the P&G Matrix, Product Supply has a different reporting line, with the additional excuse that an Arabic speaker would be better. But that went against everything I believe about leadership. Since things could turn ugly, bodyguards were offered. I refused them. It would be seen as a sign of weakness and possibly inflame the passions (we did put guards at my home to ensure the safety of my family). Whilst some threats of violence were received, the whole operation was handled peacefully and in a respectful way.

3. **One simple habit to acquire is to 'Go and See'.**

Claude L. Meyer, a legendary President (Ret.) of P&G's European Fabric Care division, always did a storecheck before any management review. He'd go on his own to avoid seeing 'prepared' stores. It's a good idea to meet with teams and consumers, to experience reality first-hand. Be seen in the trenches (if only more generals had done that in the muddy killing fields of Ypres and Passchendaele during WWI).

4. **The line of communication is not the same as the line of command.**

The line of command must be respected. Once a decision is made (after an open and frank debate), all must execute it to the best of their ability without slacking, backstabbing, and second-guessing.

However, communication can jump ranks. It's vital because the higher up in the hierarchy, the less you will be exposed to bad news. Good news will get to you in nanoseconds. Failures will be covered up or sugar-coated. You should feel free to contact anybody in the organization to get information without going through all the layers. It will also keep your direct reports honest if they know you have access to other sources of data. As mentioned, Go and See.

5. Build 'heart'.

In an interview with Colonel Sharon Gat, who commanded Israeli Special Forces, I've asked about the quality he rates the highest in his team.[2] Without hesitation, he answered: 'Heart'. He explained that when you must run into a wall of enemy fire, you lead. But you also want guys to follow you with the same determination because they have heart. It's built by the full implementation of the Mission Success Equation.

6. Make the sum bigger than the individual parts (be The Beatles and The Rolling Stones).

We talked earlier about the enduring success of U2 in an industry where most bands fail after a couple of years. It also has to do with team composition and sticking with a team that works, warts and all. Paul McCartney, John Lennon, George Harrison, and Ringo Starr released good albums after their split from The Beatles. But none of their work matches 'Revolver' or 'Sgt. Pepper's'. Together they were the Fab Four, the best pop group ever. In The Beatles, the sum was bigger than the individual parts (still my favourite definition of diversity). That's what you want in your team. Of course, if the sum is smaller, it's time to make some team changes.

As stated before, people are not your biggest asset. The right people are. Who was the first drummer of The Beatles? Pete Best. He was replaced by Ringo. Mr. Best was fired after the first recording sessions and thus narrowly missed superstardom. The band felt Best was not good enough. Manager Brian Epstein made the hard call and ultimately decided that

'If the group was to remain happy, Pete Best must go.' You certainly know Mick Jagger and Keith Richards. Ever heard of Ian 'Stu' Stewart? He was one of the founding members of the Rolling Stones and an outstanding piano player. Mr. Stewart was asked to leave the band early on. The excuse was that six members in a band was too much. The real reason was that manager Andrew Loog Oldham felt Stu's face and image did not match the band's cool 'anti-Beatles' bad boy look. Were both bands right to make these changes? I think so. The Beatles without Ringo would not have been the same. The Stones did bank heavily on their image (recall the tagline: 'Would you let your daughter marry a Rolling Stone?'). It's part of the leader's job to make the hard people calls.

One often overlooked issue is that VUCA is not just external but often internal. When discussing VUCA, people tend to point at creative disruption by competitors, wars, earthquakes, all things that happen outside of the office. But it can be internal as well. For instance, sometimes executives in the team dislike each other intensely. Should it be the case, then it makes managing a business crisis much more difficult to do. The crisis might merely serve as a tool to finish off a rival. Lots of energy will be used directly for that purpose. One more reason to make the required hard people calls before any business issue appears.

The sum of things can be fragile. If it's there, hold on to it. Even if it means compromise. Some bands understand that. Mick Jagger and Keith Richards of The Rolling Stones have a very troubled relationship. But they are wise enough to understand that together – and only together – they are the Glimmer Twins, part of the biggest rock band of all time. U2 also struggled, with bass player Adam Clayton. Mr. Clayton was an addict. Things came to a head when he missed a stadium show in November 1993 in Sydney. Luckily guitar technicians are often as good – if not better – musicians and someone could jump in for Clayton. Yet, U2 stuck with him. Following rehab, Clayton is back on track.

The Clash did not stand by their addicted drummer, 'Topper' Headon. He was asked to go after another unsuccessful rehab. Topper had become hard to handle. Yet, singer Joe Strummer admitted that firing Topper was the beginning of the end for the band. Once they had broken the close unit that delivered their artistic highs (*London Calling* is a masterpiece), something was irrecoverably lost.

Never forget that success is often linked to the talent of others, to some chemistry that is hard to define. No matter how good we are, we have strengths and weak spots. Seek team members who can cover the latter areas. Recruit people who are better than yourself.

7. Publish a leader's compass.[3]

The leader's compass is exactly that: a one-pager listing the core values that guide you. It's in the stormy weather of VUCA that the compass is the most valuable. It has two advantages: (a) people will know what drives you and consequently better understand your actions. (b) By publishing it, you are committed. Not living up to the list will get you branded a fake by the organization.

8. Be ready to acknowledge your mistakes.

> Here's one of mine. At some point in Morocco, we launched a low-priced detergent brand, Bonux. This was done before all the formula issues on Tide were properly diagnosed. As a result, the brand suffered from the same product issues and was quickly delisted. I made it worse. As background it is important to know that the global packaging design of Tide is orange whilst Bonux is red. The locals warned me that in Arabic the word for orange and red is the same. Therefore, in areas with high illiteracy, Bonux would be confused for Tide and cannibalize Tide a lot. As was their wont, consumers would ask for the 'red' pack, which could mean Tide or Bonux. I did not listen. In my defence, P&G Morocco had missed a lot of great global initiatives by 'non-invented here syndrome'. I did not want to deviate from the global standard again. Big mistake. No excuse. There was lots of consumer confusion. The locals were right.

EXECUTIVE SUMMARY

1. Choose the harder right versus the easier wrong.
2. Practice leadership from the front.
3. Go and see.
4. The line of communication is not the same as the line of command.
5. Build 'heart' in the organization.
6. Make the sum bigger than the individual parts in your team. Dare to make the tough people calls.
7. Publish a leader's compass.
8. Be ready to acknowledge your mistakes.

UNDERSTANDING
KNOW YOUR BUBBLES

Let's go back to the P&G Morocco case. Top brand Tide was in serious trouble. Volume was halved. Consumers were leaving the franchise in droves. There was a tug of war between Marketing and R&D. Marketeers kept saying that women (in Morocco, laundry was exclusively a female business) complained about lack of suds and harshness on hands because 'Tide is like stones'. R&D disagreed. They performed a simple test to prove that Tide delivered plenty of bubbles. They took two buckets, added competitor Omo in one and Tide in the other. By simply spinning the water by hand, lots of suds were generated by both brands. Ergo, the issue must be found in the marketing programs. Actually, both departments were wrong when the issue was researched in depth.

Moroccans use a very specific process to do the laundry. A bit of powder is mixed with water and kneaded into a paste. Some paste is then put on the garment and rubbed on a washing board (the kind skiffle bands use for rhythm). It is at that specific moment – when the rubbing hits the board – that foam must be seen. Suds are also believed to have a lubricating effect. Work on a board is harsh on hands. Tide did not deliver enough suds at that moment, the moment that truly mattered. If paste is left over, it gets stored and re-used at a later date.

Water is then again added to remake the paste. Tide paste was by then partly hardened, did not dissolve properly, and indeed contained hard nuggets, 'like stones'. Rubbing with that paste was harsh on hands. Once the issue was properly understood, R&D, with the local and regional team, delivered a brilliant product that brought the business back.

1. Understanding can be reached by a very simple three letter word: WHY? That's all it takes. Plus, the willingness to ask the question in the first place of course (and to listen to answers you may not like).
    - Why are social media successful? Did you not have friends before Facebook, jobs before LinkedIn, or a partner prior to dating sites?
    - Why is there huge income inequality amongst musicians but a lot less amongst heart surgeons?

The answers are out there. All that's required is to search for them. Taiichi Ohno, the engineer considered the father of the Toyota Production System (a.k.a. Lean Production) introduced the '5 Whys Method'. He saw it as the basis for Toyota's scientific approach: 'by repeating 'why?' five times, the nature of the problem as well as its solution becomes clear'.[1]

2. **Set up a compulsory 'in touch' program for employees.**

Everybody must participate in it. Yes, also the people who do the accounting, agency creatives and senior executives. It can be shop-a-longs. Just join a consumer on a shopping trip and observe what happens. In-home visits can teach one a lot. How do people live? What's important to them? Employees will come back with loads of insights. What's the incremental cost of spending a day in a supermarket to learn from consumers? Zero.

> At P&G Morocco, we created 'Les Musts de P&G'. Employees could choose to be a 'missionary' for a day. The name is inspired by the Jesuit motto of 'one soul at a time'. Each consumer matters. The job was to stand next to the laundry shelf in a supermarket. Every time somebody picked a competitive brand, they'd ask why. Why not Tide or Ariel? 'Missionaries' were also given a small cash budget. They could decide to fund a trial pack to help convince a competitive user. Or one could be a 'streetfighter' and join one of the Sales vans. Their objective was to improve the shelf presence of the Laundry portfolio.

Here's an insight from one of my Moroccan in-home visits. I asked a mother from a poor family what the hardest part of her life was. I had expected an answer about not being able to afford many material things. She said: 'That we do not count'. ***There's a vital leadership lesson in there: always preserve the dignity of others, no matter who they are.***

3. Manage by asking questions.

It's the essence of Socratic dialogue. Instead of stating an opinion, ask a question to your team. The answer may surprise you and make you change your mind. You can always still express your point of view later and stick to your guns. Questions are seen as less threatening and create higher involvement. Reports do not always need to win the argument (well most don't...) but enjoy the fact that they were given a chance to advocate their view. Finally, it is a good teaching method. People always believe things more when they figure out the logic of an argument by themselves. Some might say that this leads to time loss in meetings. Yes, it might. But the benefits more than compensate for it. Sometimes productivity has to yield to another valuable objective.

4. An essential prerequisite is that people feel safe to speak up: create an intellectual democracy.

I went as far as to define a 'constitution'. Some of the rules included:
- Facts win. If the new hire has them, they overrule the CEO. The consumer is boss.
- Allow people to get facts. Therefore, give resources for market research but within an agreed methodology to avoid chaos.
- All can – nay must – speak their mind. It's safe to do so.
- Once a decision is reached, we act as one.
- In the 'After Action Review', 6 to 12 months later, we can re-evaluate our decision. If any of us were wrong: own it, learn from it.

5. Ensure continuity.

Experience does matter. It takes time and effort to understand a business. Consequently, it is good to ensure that there is sufficient continuity in staffing. By all means, throw in some new blood but keep the core of deep industry knowledge intact. P&G used to have the rule to only change one thing at a time in a person's career track: either the country, the type of business or the level, but never all three at the same time. This also increased the chances of the employee to succeed in the new assignment.

Continuity also creates what Malcom Gladwell calls 'Blink', the ability to see in the blink of an eye if something fits or not.[2] Mr. Claude Meyer, whom we met earlier, could judge quickly whether a piece of detergent advertising was right or not. Looking at an Ariel detergent commercial for 30 seconds, he'd be able to say: 'It's not Ariel.'
'Why not?'
'It's just not Ariel'.
After that initial gut feeling, logical arguments were provided. Often, consumer research would support his judgment. Claude did not have paranormal powers. What he did have was 25 years of category experience.

EXECUTIVE SUMMARY:

1. Be curious and ask 'why'.
2. Set up a compulsory 'in touch' programme for employees.
3. Manage by asking questions.
4. An essential prerequisite is that people feel safe to speak up: create an intellectual democracy.
5. Make sure to have continuity to preserve deep industry knowledge.

RESILIENCE

JOIN THE NEVER GIVE UP CLUB

≡ The power or ability to recover readily from adversity, from being bent, compressed, or stretched, elasticity.

Mr. Paul Stanley is testament to the power of resilience. Born with microtia, a birth defect causing the absence or deformity of the external ear, he was deaf on his right side. Despite being bullied as a child and called 'the one-eared monster', Stanley believes this harsh experience fuelled his drive to become a superstar. As the lead singer and guitarist of KISS, he assumed the persona of 'the Starchild' and went on to lead the iconic band to sell over 100 million albums, 14 of which achieved platinum status. His net worth is estimated at $200m.[1]

1. **Morale of the story: adversity can be turned into a source of strength.**

Adventurer, TV star and ex-Elite Special Forces soldier (SAS) Bear Grylls advises to write the following on our bathroom mirror: 'Struggle develops strength and storms make us stronger.'[2] It's a take on philosopher Nietzsche's adage: 'That which does not kill us, makes us stronger' (though it does not always feel like that when one is knee deep in trouble…).

What do The Beatles, Dr. Seuss and John Grisham have in common? They were all rejected. Mr. Grisham's first novel no less than 28 times, Dr. Seuss' first story 27 times. Equally, many business leaders did not win all the time. Several CEOs were fired at some point in their career. Steve Jobs was. Elon Musk was twice ousted as CEO (at Zip2 and PayPal). As the song goes: 'Everybody's gotta learn sometime': to cope with losing, how to rebound and to adsorb hard lessons from failing. Despite the rejections, they all kept going. As we say in karate: *'A black belt is a white belt that never gave up.'*

An interesting question from a student: 'But is there not a time when it is wise to give up?' Yes, there is. Let's take the case of metal band Anvil. Anvil is a Canadian metal band that showed promise in the early 80s. They developed a sound that influenced the big four (Metallica, Anthrax, Megadeth, Slayer). However, Anvil quickly disappeared from the limelight. An ex-roadie sought them out in 2008 and made a film about their story. The movie was a major hit and made the band famous in extremis.

What's most interesting however is what Anvil did in those 25 years of obscurity. Basically, they made the same album repeatedly. After each flop, they recorded ten similar albums with similar lyrics and sleeve designs. They did not seem to question that a different image and better song-writing talent were needed. Anvil certainly deserve kudos for sheer stubbornness and determination. But, as mentioned earlier, we do need to learn from failure and dare to question ourselves in the absence of success. ***One cannot expect different results by doing the same thing.*** The band was only rescued from total oblivion by a lucky shot.

Triathlete Mark Allen took a different approach. He was one of the first to get into this discipline. Despite training hard, he did not complete his first Iron Man in 1982. For two years thereafter, he pushed himself harder and harder in training. However, results did not improve. Then he met Dr. Phil Maffletone who coached him to make a change and to train differently. By 1995, Mr. Allen had won six Iron Man competitions and is considered one of the top endurance athletes of all time.[3] This proves that whilst we need to be resilient, we should also be smart about it.

> ***There can be opportunity in adversity.*** I was on my way home in Casablanca. Tomorrow was the big day. After months of preparation, we were ready to present the critical restructuring plan to the Moroccan government's highest echelons. It was going to be a challenge for reasons explained earlier. Whilst driving, I got an urgent call from my External Relations manager with the request to watch the CNN channel as soon as I could. Upon arrival home, I promptly did and saw a plane fly into the Twin Towers in NYC. The date was September 11, 2001. What now? Should we postpone the restructuring's announcement? After a call with the American embassy, it was decided to delay. We immediately also saw opportunity. There was a serious risk of sabotage in the plants when the restructuring would be announced. However, we had not been able to put on additional security. Such action would have prematurely alarmed the all-powerful unions that something was up before we were ready. However,

following 9/11 everyone thought it only appropriate that we put on more security personnel. There had already been rumours about a possible restructuring. But now for two crucial weeks, all talk was about 9/11.

2. Get purpose.

≡ The intention to contribute to the well-being of others.

This is the very bedrock of resilience. Nietzsche put it best: 'He who has a Why to live for can bear almost any How.'

Purpose strengthens resolve. If one asks Israelis why their country exists, the vast majority answer: 'to create a safe place for Jews'. Consequently, many are willing to fight and sacrifice for their country. Sometimes I ask audiences: 'Why does Belgium exist?' If any response is given at all, it can be summed up as 'chocolate' or 'mussels and fries'. In an international survey the question was raised: 'Would you be willing to defend your motherland, knowing that you might die in the process?' In Belgium, a mere 19% answered positively. That makes sense. The country has no well-defined purpose. Few want to die for mussels and fries (not for Gouda cheese either: the Netherlands, 15%). In case you are wondering, Finland scored the highest in Europe at 74%. They've proven it too against overwhelming force when Stalin invaded in 1939.[4]

Purpose can help you survive the very worst. The experience of Viennese psychologist Viktor Frankl, author of the celebrated *Man's Search for Meaning*, confirms the power of meaning.[5] Mr. Frankl survived the horror of the Nazi death camps. Out of that terrible experience came his theory of logotherapy.[*]

---

* From the Greek 'Logos' which connotes 'meaning'.

Whilst a prisoner, he wanted to understand what optimized the chances of survival. The key finding was that as soon as a prisoner lost faith in the future – his future – he was doomed. Those who kept faith and an expectation of what they had to offer to life had stronger resilience. They found strength in beliefs such as:

> 'If I do not survive, my daughter will never have a father.'
> 'If I do not carry on, then this novel will never be written.'
> 'If I do not make it out of here alive, then the cure I was working on might never benefit mankind.'

Frankl saw three possible sources of meaning: in work (doing something significant), in love, and in 'courage in suffering'. He based his therapy on a vital insight: that conditions can take everything away from you except one thing: your freedom to choose how you will respond to the situation. Mr. Frankl's views echo those of the Stoics.* They believed that every person is given a spark of divinity and that nobody – not even the gods – can take it away.

The English band The The (this is not a typo, they were really called that) expressed the thought in a great song line: 'If you cannot change the world around you, change the world inside of you.'

How do we find purpose? A good starting point is this wonderful definition of purpose: *'the place where your talent meets the needs of the world'*. Said differently, what is it that only your company can do and what can it do better than anybody else that benefits others? Why do we exist? It's important to

---

* Stoicism is a school of Hellenistic philosophy founded by Zeno of Citium in Athens in the early 3rd century BC.

ensure a link to your activities. Purpose is not the same as charity (noble as that is). Once defined, purpose becomes the yardstick for everything the company does. Three important watch-outs must be mentioned:

a) <u>Make sure the purpose does not become airy-fairy</u>. Avoid a disconnect from the core business. The business is the very engine that allows you to achieve the purpose. As such it is not in contradiction with a profit motive.

b) <u>Purpose is not the same as politics</u>. Gillette had a great purpose to make men look and feel their best. Those my age may remember the very first 'The best a man can get' ad. It was a magnificent celebration of male virtues: courage, bonding, achievement, ambition, loyalty. More recently, the company aired 'toxic masculinity' ads. Negative comments were 10 to 1 versus positives.[6]

c) <u>Don't forget the short term</u>. To achieve the goal of making a positive impact on the world, it is often important to deliver compelling shorter-term results as well. If not, one risks losing support of the Board and shareholders. As quoted by a CEO, 'the long term is many quarters in a row.'

3. Build 'grit' & willpower.

Consider these two stories: On January 18, 1915, British explorer Ernest Shackleton's ship got into trouble. The aptly named *Endurance* froze in the icy waters of the coast of Antarctica. For months, the ice pressed against the sturdy ship until on October 28 floes snapped the hull. Shackleton's crew had no choice but to seek refuge on the ice. Following incredible adventures that challenge belief, intense suffering in one of the world's most inhospitable places, in an age without satellite phones, antibiotics or helicopter search teams, the crew were rescued on August 30, 1916. Every single one of them had survived the ordeal. A lot of the credit goes to Mr. Shackleton whose leadership qualities came to the fore and saved the proverbial day.[7]

Freddy Spencer Chapman was an artic explorer, naturalist and soldier who became trapped behind enemy lines when the Japanese overran Malaya in 1942. He started his own guerrilla campaign. He was mercilessly hunted, wounded, nearly destroyed by tropical disease, captured, and escaped. His companions were less lucky. They were beheaded. Mr. Chapman held out for three years and five months in the jungle. He was all alone most of the time.[8]

As one reads these stories, the question comes to mind: where does that incredible level of grit come from? Do these people possess supernatural powers? Angela Duckworth, Professor of Psychology at the University of Pennsylvania, made it her mission to find out. *The secret of 'grit' lies in a combination of passion and perseverance.*[9]

a) *Passion is not enthusiasm but is defined in terms of consistency over time.* Everybody who has gone camping knows that enthusiasm dies out rather quickly when a rainstorm drenches all and sundry. Passion is built on four key components:
   i. <u>Enjoying what you do</u>. Why should we love our jobs? One could say that it's obviously nicer to get out of

bed in the morning to go and do something one likes. But there is another profound reason.

ii. <u>The resilience to practice</u>. Only those who like what they do are willing to put up with the often tedious, endless repetitions required to become truly good at something. Our parents were right: practice makes perfect.

iii. <u>Purpose</u>. Another way to define your purpose is via following the advice Congresswoman Claire Boothe Luce offered to President John F. Kennedy. She told him: 'A great man is a sentence.' Abraham Lincoln's was: 'He preserved the nation and freed the slaves.'[10]

iv. <u>Hope</u>. It's important to believe that we can get to where we want to get to. One could argue that it can be a bit irrational. There can only be one winner in the 100 m sprint during the Olympics. If one of the contenders was Jamaican sprinter Usain Bolt, it's surely not realistic to believe that one could win. Yet, without hope, one should not even participate. It certainly would be impossible to sustain the gruelling training regimen to make it to an Olympic final in the first place.

b) ***Perseverance is linked to willpower.*** Self-control and discipline are key to success. If it can be merged with purpose, one gets transformation. Sometimes, in seminars, I hear: 'Well, I just do not have discipline.' To which I reply: 'Where do you plan on buying it? In the supermarket? Order it via Amazon?' We can only find it in ourselves. There may not be an 'I' in 'team' but there certainly is in 'willpower'. The good news is that we can strengthen willpower. Here are a couple of insights:

i. <u>Set only one – 1 – clear goal at the time.</u> As we all know, setting goals is not enough. If it were, we'd have no issue delivering on our New Year's resolutions. In fact, in the USA, only 13% of people succeed in sticking to them. One of the reasons is that we put far too much on the list. It's better to be choiceful. Why?
ii. <u>You only have a finite amount of willpower that becomes depleted as you use it.</u> That's why after a day of rigorously sticking to a diet, we ruin it in the evening in front of the TV with a massive ice-cream splurge fest. The willpower supply had run out.
iii. <u>You can only use the stock of willpower for the tasks you choose.</u>[11] Said differently, if you use up your supply for dieting, you may not have anything left to deal with something else. Even unrelated activities draw on the same source.
iv. <u>The willpower supply can be made bigger. Seemingly unrelated activities that require willpower and discipline increase it</u>. This is a wonderful thing. In one experiment, students were divided into two groups. One group was asked to sit up straight. The other group was asked nothing at all. Two weeks later, lab tests on self-control showed significantly higher scores for the first group. By overriding the habit of slouching, students got stronger willpower and did better at tasks that had nothing to do with how they sat.[12]

P&G Morocco also needed a shot of discipline. To get there, we banned jeans in the general office. Not because there's anything wrong with a pair of Levi's but to drive a different culture. Name badges were to be visibly worn.

If forgotten at home, one had to immediately leave the office to get it. Some employees would protest: 'but you know me'. True, the badge rule by itself was meaningless as I knew all the employees. But this small act, like the no jeans rule, was designed to set the tone for discipline in other projects. It really works that way. At the start, it was not exactly popular. But as a couple of months passed by, lots of people expressed their gratitude for the higher standards and rigor.

v. <u>Willpower eats up energy. Fuel up with glucose</u>. Let's review the curious case of the four men in Israeli prisons requesting parole. They had very similar profiles. All were repeat offenders, had already done jail time before, had served two-thirds of their current sentence, and qualified for a rehabilitation program if released. There was one major difference though: two of them were Jewish Israeli and two Arab Israeli. The verdict was very different for each prisoner. Some were released and some not. Your gut probably gives you a feeling on how you think the decisions went. It was indeed a question of gut. But it had absolutely nothing to do with ethnicity. The findings from this case were further validated in an analysis of more than 1000 parole board decisions by a team of psychologists led by Jonathan Levav of Columbia University and Shai Danziger of Ben-Gurion University. On average, one out of three prisoners received parole. The startling finding however was that those who appeared early in the morning received a positive ruling about 70% of the time. Those whose turn came late in the day less than 10%. A deeper analysis of how the day went, showed the same remarkable pattern. At 10.30am the board took a food break. Those who appeared just before that break got a 20% chance of parole. Those who came after it, had a 65% chance. Guess what? The same happened just before and after lunch. Decision-making is hard work. It consumes lots of energy. When the glucose tank was empty, like before a food break, judges preferred not to grant parole because their willpower was depleted. The easy decision was just to say 'no' and move on. When the tank was full, the hard decision to grant parole was easier to make. Lady Justice is blind but only provided she is well fed.[13]

vi. <u>Create a habit</u>. We'll cover that in the Change Management Pillar.

4. Cultivate a growth 'mindset.'

We owe a lot to the brilliant insights of Dr. Carol S. Dweck, Professor of Psychology at Stanford. The publisher's boast on her book's backflap that it has changed millions of lives is no hyperbole.[14] I confess that it affected mine. For instance, when asked if I'm a good guitar player, I used to answer: 'I'm very average, I have no talent'. Now I say: 'I never put in the effort to practice hard enough' (still as average though). ***There are two types of mindsets: (a) the fixed or 'talent' mindset and (b) the growth mindset***. The way you adopt one or the other determines the way you lead your life.

a) ***The fixed mindset drives the belief that our qualities are set in stone***. We are given a fixed amount of talent and must make do with that. We only have a certain amount of intelligence, a certain personality, so much moral character, so much willpower, a certain style. You may have heard this one in relationships when making a comment about something you did not like about your partner: 'Well, that's just the way I am.' Fixed mindset people in romantic relationships expect to be put on a pedestal, including humble worship at their feet.

People with a fixed mindset deal badly with feedback. It is seen as personal criticism. Failure is associated with identity: I AM a failure. They also believe that anybody who expends lots of effort in any given activity probably did not have any talent to start with.

Usually, bosses with a fixed mindset tend not to be pleasant ones because of a need to prove themselves in any situation. 'How will I look?' is an obsession. They feel threatened by people who are better. As a matter of fact, the worse other people look, the better. Because then these bosses stand out by comparison.

b) *The growth mindset is based on the belief that we can cultivate our basic qualities by effort and the help of others.* Our talent is just the starting point. This does not mean that you or I could be Jimi Hendrix. But it does mean that with hard work and motivation, we can get much better.

The growth mindset is convinced that our true potentials are unknown and there's no saying what we could achieve with dedication and effort. That's why the pages covering the childhood and teenage years in the biographies of rock & roll stars are usually quite boring. Most of the time it's ordinary stuff. Sometimes, by most standards, these kids would be considered failures: school dropouts, lousy school results. But then by hard work, and meeting up with other musicians, magic happens.

Darwin's talent did not initially come to light either, yet he became one of the most influential scientists ever. In his youth, he dropped out of med school. His father was furious and wrote: 'You care for nothing but shooting, dogs and rat-catching, and you will be a disgrace to yourself and all your family.'[15]

In the growth mindset, feedback is welcomed as a gift. Failure is seen as an action: 'I HAVE failed' and leads to the reflection on how the experience can become a source of growth and learning. Leaders operating in this space have no issue recruiting people who are exceptionally gifted and might become better than them.

Mindset is a personal decision. What's yours?

5. Manage your energy.

This section is not about how you look or weight loss. It is about energy. Jim Citrin, who leads executive search firm Spencer Stuart's CEO practice, has this advice for newly promoted senior leaders: 'This is going to be a sprint that's going to be the first leg of what's going to be a marathon. So, you have to manage your energy level.' Energy is a key feature of resilience. There are different sources of energy (figure 21).

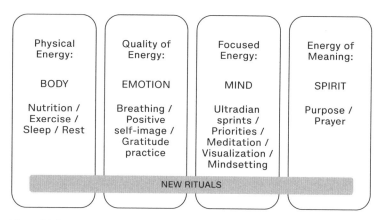

Figure 21: Energy Management (Based on Jim Loehr & Tony Schwartz, 'The Making of a Corporate Athlete', HBR, Reprint R01010H / Tony Schwartz, 'Manage Your Energy, Not Your Time', HBR, October 2007, and personal attendance at 'Corporate Athlete' Seminars

a) Body: physical energy is at the core.

'Mens sana in corpore sano' (a healthy mind in a healthy body) knew the Ancients. Unilever insisted that every subsidiary with more than 200 employees installed a fitness centre.[16] There's no secret to how to become fit. It's a combination of exercise, nutrition, and rest. There's not one training system to recommend but a mixture of strength, endurance and flexibility typically serves well. A couple of suggestions:

i. **Your body suffices as a fitness centre.** You do not need a fancy place, nor spend more time away from home and family. Special Forces training regimens are nearly all based on own body weight, composed of classics such as burpees, sit-ups, push-ups, lunges, squats, pull-ups, and the like. You can practice them anywhere and at zero cost. Add some running.

ii. **Your kids may be the best exercise equipment.** They just love to sit on your back whilst you do push-ups.

They enjoy being lifted in the air. What a great bargain! You'll be fit and kids will rate you the coolest parent on the planet.
    iii. *It takes only 30 minutes, four times a week.* Just doing that will transform your body. Legal disclaimer: exercise responsibly in line with your abilities and age.
    iv. *Feed the beast*: No glucose, no power. The fuel you put into your body drives, or depletes, energy. Do inform yourself on this in depth.
    v. *Have a yearly check-up.* It's a good idea to do a full check-up every year, certainly after the age of 40. It has the added advantage of potentially giving you some hard 'wake-up call' data on indicators such as cholesterol.
    vi. *Recovery time is not weakness.* Rasmus Ankersen is an expert on high performance. In his studies on what makes for top athletes, he found that deliberately investing time in energy renewal is important. Surprisingly, Mr. Ankersen found that top performers also slept more. 'You must not only train like a champ, but you must also sleep like one'.[17]

b) Quality, emotional energy.
    i. *Expressing gratitude helps.* It may be as simple as saying grace before each family dinner. Even if one is not religious, it is good practice. You might do it via a Yoga sun salutation exercise in the morning to welcome life. You can simply say: 'another day alive, great' as soon as you get out of bed.
    ii. *A positive self-image is a good thing as well.* The stories we tell ourselves matter.

iii. ***Take a breath.*** Commander Mark Divine, a retired Navy SEAL, founder of SEALFIT and the Unbeatable Mind Academy believes that learning breath control is the most important component of forging mental toughness. One simple technique is 'box breathing'. Start by exhaling all air from your lungs. Then inhale to the count of five and hold your breath for five counts. Exhale to the count of five and hold for another five. Doing this for five to ten minutes each day is enough. Divine suggests also adding a power mantra or jingle in your mind.[18]

c) The focused Mind.
   i. ***Mindsetting is excellent mental preparation.*** It's surprising that training on how to survive violent crime does not recommend learning karate or to carry pepper spray. Rather, one of the most important principles is 'mindsetting', which refers to mental preparation and rehearsal.[19] We've opened this book with a terrorist attack. We never think through such a scenario beforehand, nor do we involve our families in such an exercise. So, when it happens, we are likely to freeze and feel helpless. Yet, we have all practiced mindsetting in our heads extensively. We do it before asking for a raise, a promotion or to convince somebody to date us. Before making a move, we:
- visualize ourselves in the situation;
- visualize our actions;
- think through objections and rejection. 'If the boss says this, I'll answer that'.

The reason why mindsetting works is that it creates patterns of preparedness. When something happens or we are faced with adversity, we know how to act with a focused mind and are not paralyzed or left clueless. As will be covered below in point 5, building muscle memory on top makes for better execution when the moment comes.

    ii. *Visualization of the desired outcome is important.* It means creating a mental picture of your future state or success and to hold that firmly in your mind. Put differently: *win in your mind first.*

    iii. *Meditation is a time-honored method to achieve focus.* It's been around for at least 5000 years, possibly longer. The mind is like water. If you keep it still, it will settle.

    iv. *Full engagement expert Tony Schwarz also recommends 'ultradian sprints'.* The idea is to fully focus for 90 to 120 minutes and then take a real break.[20] It's hard to focus beyond that duration. Hence, it is good to build meeting agendas and to-do lists around 90-minute cycles. The break matters too as it allows for renewal.

d) The inner power of the unbeatable spirit:

    i. *As covered above, purpose provides meaning and is a tremendous source of inner power.* If you are still in search of it, you may want to watch the delightful TED talk on YouTube called 'How to Know Your Life Purpose in 5 Minutes'. Speaker Mr. Adam Leipzig asks you to consider five questions:
- Who are you?
- What do you do?
- Who do you do it for?
- Why do they need what you do?
- How are they transformed by what you do?

Note that three of the questions are not about you but about other people.

ii. ***Regular religious practice makes a difference too.*** In secular countries, it often gets bad press and is rated as 'delusional'. But it does generate a long list of positives, from fewer social ills to increased personal and mental health.[21] The psychologist Michael McCullough (who is not religiously devout), looked at over 30 studies that asked people about their religious devotion and kept track of them over time. It turned out that non-religious people died sooner. At any given point, a religiously active person was 25% more likely to be alive than a non-religious one. It is not so much a question of divine intervention as it is of having better habits. Less of the things that may be fun but are not entirely beneficial to health such as drug abuse, risky sex, and smoking. More of the responsible things such as seatbelt usage, taking vitamins and regular dentist visits.[22] So, if you get ridiculed for your religious beliefs, know that you may have the last laugh. Literally.

All the above may require new habits, new rituals. Everybody has lots of habits. We may as well create some good ones.

6. Build muscle memory.

How do we respond to the monthly fire drill? Typically, by moaning. 'I was just in an important customer call!' Next, we gather possessions even though we've been instructed to leave everything behind and get out quickly. It's a human trait. Then we walk out in a leisurely fashion, chatting merrily with colleagues.

Rick Rescorla would have none of it. Mr. Rescorla was head of security of Morgan Stanley Dean Witter in the NYC World Trade Center ('WTC'). He had expressed misgivings about the security in the WTC early on. Having consulted an anti-terror expert, he warned that a truck full of explosives might be driven into the building's car park. That warning was ignored, just as Rescorla was when he tried to run fire drills at Morgan Stanley.

On February 26, 1993, a Pakistani terrorist (Ramzi Yousef) did exactly what was feared. A 680 kg car bomb was detonated below Tower One. It failed to bring the towers down but cost the lives of six people and injured over 1000. Rescorla learnt from that. He had seen what happened to the average employee on that occasion. He noticed the initial denial, the time lag to finally get into action and the slowness of the evacuation. Rescorla feared another attack would eventually come and decided to prep the organization. He'd run surprise and radical fire drills with very clear instructions. It made him very unpopular in a company full of alpha types, but he persevered.

On the morning of September 11, 2001, Rescorla heard an explosion and saw a fire in Tower One. A Port Authority official urged all on the public address system to stay at their desks. Rescorla ignored it and shot into action. He ordered an immediate evacuation. It went smoothly because muscle memory had been built. In a disaster, the brains of an untrained person shut down. The only way to get it to perform in extreme stress is to run it through rehearsals beforehand. Rescorla had created bookmarks in people's head, so they had an action map to fall back on. The action steps had become what we call 'second nature'. 2687 employees made it out safely. 13 did not. One of them was Rick Rescorla. Upon hearing that some people were missing, he raced back into the building only to have the tower collapse on him. The remains of this hero were never found.[23]

Remember Operation White Angels when terrorists hijacked a Sabena Plane, and held it at Tel Aviv airport? One of the first things that was done, was to get the same model plane. It was put in a remote area of the airport. The commandos begun rehearsing a coordinated entry through both the pilot's cockpit and emergency exits, in order to build muscle memory. The techniques practiced allowed them to neutralize the terrorists before they could trigger the explosive charges.[24]

We need to practice scenarios before the crisis happens. Make a list of key possible disruptors and drill the response to them. A major risk faced by organizations today is the possibility of a cyberattack. However, in my entire career I have never participated in a company drill to practice how to handle such a situation. All elite soldiers I've interviewed told me the same thing when I asked them how they manage volatility: 'We train incredibly hard and for the worst. Then reality isn't so bad.' Seneca, the Roman Stoic philosopher, and adviser in the early reign of the Roman emperor Nero, concluded:

> *'Everyone faces up more bravely to a thing for which he has long prepared himself, sufferings, even, being withstood if they have trained for it in advance. Those who are unpre-*

pared, on the other hand, are panic-stricken by the most insignificant happenings. We must see to it that nothing takes us by surprise.'[25]

7. Invest in the emotional bank account of your network.

When you are in a quagmire, it will feel mighty good when there is somebody to drag you out of it. Inevitably, there will be moments in your business career when things are not going well. It is therefore wise to create a support network and to make deposits in other people's emotional bank account.[26] One day you may need to draw funds from that account. Of course, if you never make deposits, do not expect anybody to help you; certainly not in times of trouble. In any case, many prefer to walk around an issue in a wide circle so as not to be tainted by it. A strong network builds resilience and acts as a possible insurance policy. Deposits can take many shapes. You can proactively help others. As the Romans said: 'Do ut des'. I give so you might give at some point in the future. If you know that somebody loves biographies, why not send a great one you discovered recently? Acts of kindness are their own reward. They provide spiritual energy.

8. Keep the focus external, especially during a crisis.

It's interesting to review the response of both Stalin and Hitler in WWII when things went badly. Both were mass murderers and evil dictators. Stalin badly misjudged Hitler's intentions in 1941. To the last minute, he believed Germany would not attack. Lest we forget, they had made a pact in 1939 and carved up Poland. When the Nazi invasion came on June 22, the Soviets suffered devastating losses. The Russian army had an initial weakness in command and leadership. Stalin had shot most senior experienced officers in the purges and show trials of the 1930s. On top, political commissars had a stranglehold on the troops. The political correctness led to sterility in strategy and tactics. Yet in the face of mounting losses, Stalin started – albeit grudgingly – to defer and delegate to others. He was lucky to have a Marshall of genius, Georgy Zhukov, and the equally capable Staff officer Aleksei Antonov. They lessened the impact of ideology and quickly learned from the tactics of the Wehrmacht. Hitler did nothing of the kind. With the war taking a turn for the worse for Nazi Germany, he progressively centralized decision-making to himself. He even argued about minor things, including how many meters a defensive line should be kept from the enemy. The Führer fired the highly capable von Manstein and Guderian. Both men had the guts to talk back, which made them vulnerable (when Hitler started shouting, Field Marshall von Manstein told him icily that he did not accept it 'because I, *I* am a gentleman').

The risk is that, when trouble hits, there is a tendency towards internal focus and centralization when it should move towards more external focus and agility. As mentioned before, it is in a crisis that the truth must be spoken and accepted. One can deny reality, but it has the annoying characteristic to hit you in the face eventually.

For the record: when the war was won, Stalin got rid of most of the officers who gave him victory and resumed his old ways.

9. Keep a sense of humor and add something that gives consolation.

Here's some comic relief. Though the point is a very serious one. *A sense of humor is an essential survival trait.* Sometimes the jokes may be bitter, but they help to keep a fighting spirit. When the German army was bleeding badly at the end of the war, soldiers told this joke: *'Khaki plane? It's English. Silver plane? American. No plane? German.'*

It's up to you to decide what kind of leader you want to be, but I like those who can laugh at themselves and keep a positive outlook (of course, jokes must be in good taste. It's always important to be sensitive). Here's one Ronald Reagan – who had a great sense of humor – told his Soviet counterpart, Mikhail Gorbachev, during a conference. Mr. Gorbachev reportedly rated it a good joke.

> *'An American meets a Russian. The American claims that the USA is the land of the free. "I can walk into the White House, slam the desk of the President and say: 'Mr. President, your policy is nonsense.'"*
> *"Ah", says the Russian, "but I can do the same."*
> *"Really?" asks the incredulous American.*
> *"Yes, I can walk into the Kremlin, slam the desk of the General Secretary, and say: 'The policy of the American President is nonsense.'"*

In the SAS Survival Handbook, there is a section on what to put in a survival kit. It has all the things one would expect, except for one surprising item: teabags.[27] Its only role is to boost morale. For the English, tea is some sort of magic potion. It's widely acknowledged that tea helped the nation to cope with the worst of the intense bombing of the Blitz (September 7, 1940 – May 11, 1941).[28] In British TV crime series, when the police have to give bad news to the families of victims, one of the first things one of the officers says is: 'I shall put the kettle on'. What is the equivalent of tea, of a small gesture or ritual that enhances morale, in your organization?

10. Use heroes, songs, a poem or a visual. Whatever works.

We need personal heroes. We find inspiration in their struggles and life choices. Sometimes a song or poem can give extra power. Nelson Mandela became President of South Africa in 1994. Prior to that, he was jailed for 27 years, most of them in the Robbeneiland maximum security prison. To keep up his resilience, he often recited William Ernest Henley's (1849–1903) *Invictus* poem. The last stanza says it all: *'It matters not how strait the gate, how charged with punishments the scroll, I am the master of my fate, I am the captain of my soul.'*

Sometimes, one image has that potency. At the start of 1945, a photo brought the fatigued American population back together and instilled in them a fresh resolve to continue the Pacific War. Remember that in those days the government had to ask for money to fight on via war bonds (now we're simply taxed). Because of an iconic photo taken by Joe Rosenthal on February 23, 1945, of four Marines raising the flag on Iwo Jima, the money came rolling in. It also became photography's most reproduced image.

EXECUTIVE SUMMARY:

1. Adversity must be turned into a source of strength. Join the never give up club.
2. Get purpose.
3. Build 'grit' & willpower.
4. Cultivate a 'growth mindset'.
5. Manage your energy.
6. Build muscle memory.
7. Invest in the emotional bank account of your network.
8. Keep the focus external.
9. Keep a sense of humor and add something that gives consolation.
10. Use heroes, songs and poems.

PILLAR 3

CHANGE MANAGEMENT

A.
WHY DO WE NEED CHANGE MANAGEMENT? SEX & THE RED QUEEN

Why is each one of us a unique individual? One could say: because the genes of two people are mixed into a new blend in every newborn. But this merely leads to the next question: why blend two people to make a new and different one? Nature decided not to opt for mass production, to just allow us to clone ourselves into equivalents of Ford Ts. Surely that would have been much more productive.

To find the answer we must return to The Red Queen whom we first encountered in the introduction. This is a character in the sequel to Alice in Wonderland. At some point, Alice meets her. The queen demands to run at full speed, but they never seem to make any progress. All the things around them move with them. They must run to stand still. ***This is called the Red Queen effect: time always erodes advantage.*** To quote biologist Matt Ridley: *'Evolutionary history is no different. Progress and success are always relative. When the land was unoccupied by animals, the first amphibian to emerge from the sea could get away with being slow, lumbering and fish-like. But if a fish were* *to take the land today it would be gobbled up by a passing fox as surely as a Mongol horde would be wiped out by machine guns.'*[1]

Humanity's biggest enemies are bacterial and viral infections (as the plague in the 14 century and Covid-19 demonstrated recently). Imagine these as a key looking to unlock a human. If we were all the same, a virus could wipe out all of humanity. But because the lock is constantly changed with every new child and every lock is different, it provides protection. The key does not fit every lock. Some humans are immune. They pass that genetic trait on to their children. Over time, group immunity is created, at least until the virus mutates in turn. That's why nature favoured sex. When groups without the opportunity to develop immunity were suddenly exposed to new diseases, the outcome was disastrous. It explains how a tiny band of Spanish conquistadores conquered the mighty Inca empire in Peru. Francisco Pizarro González had only 200 men and yet beat an army of thousands. True, the Spanish had superior war equipment (guns, horses, and steel) and were utterly ruthless in exploiting the naivety of Inca emperor Atahuallpa. They also had a secret weapon: germs. The local population had no defence against smallpox, measles, and influenza. Some sources estimate that up to 90% of Native Americans subsequently died.*

The Austrian economist Schumpeter coined the term 'creative destruction'. It's the process by which constant innovation drives other products and processes out of the market. *As a result, there is no such thing as a lasting competitive advantage. Change is the only constant and we must master it if we want the mission to sustainably succeed.*

---

* One can then ask the question: why did the Europeans have 'Guns, Germs and Steel'? Professor of Psychology Jared Diamond provides a compelling theory in his book with that title.

B.
WHEN TO CHANGE? WHAT BOWIE AND U2 GOT RIGHT

The fans were horrified. How could he possibly kill Ziggy Stardust! Artist David Bowie created this fictional character in 1972. The parent album *The Rise and Fall of Ziggy Stardust and the Spiders from Mars* was his commercial breakthrough (7.5 million copies sold). Mr. Bowie bade farewell to his beloved stage persona at the height of Ziggy's success in July 1973. He continued to re-invent himself in the 70s and early 80s. Bowie was respectively Aladdin Sane and the Thin White Duke. He was first to tap into the Berlin scene, and later used the New Romantics style (on the video of *Ashes to Ashes*), to eventually become blond and suntanned on his most successful album *Let's Dance* (11 million sold, not bad for a non-mainstream artist). It's because of this power of renewal and a genius to anticipate change that Bowie stayed relevant in a notoriously fickle industry.

1. Not only the music industry, but every business goes through cycles (see figure 22 below). As Harvard professor Clayton Christensen argued, these take the shape of an S-curve, a 'sigmoid' curve. Ideally, one anticipates change and creates a new growth curve when the business is still good, before the old model runs out of steam.

It's not easy because at the start there might be some lower performance driven by the 'innovator's dilemma'. Typically, a new product or process initially only delivers minimum value. It takes time to create a consumer base and sufficient scale. But doing nothing leads to stagnation and ultimately decline.

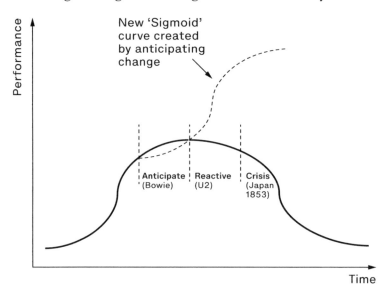

Figure 22: The Change Cycle & The Sigmoid Curve (Source: Charles Handy defined the S-curve in the 1990s. Anticipate / Reactive / Crisis based on an IMD business school model. Sigmoid curve concept introduced to me by Mr. W. Geissler)

2. **The next best time to change is when the business is in stagnation. That's a reactive response.**

The Irish rock band U2 did that. They became intergalactic superstars following the release of *The Joshua Tree* (25 million sales). Everything was right about it: the songs, the band's performance, and the sleeve design. U2 next released *Rattle and Hum*. Although 15 million copies were sold, mostly off the back of the previous album, reviews were mixed at best. Within the band as well, there was a feeling of creative stagnation. They then took the very courageous decision to record *Achtung Baby*. It was a departure from their usual style incorporating alternative and electronic sounds. Certainly, many who loved *The Joshua Tree* were disappointed. But had the band made another *Joshua Tree*, they'd have become irrelevant. Instead, they created a new 'Sigmoid' curve by tapping into a new cultural trend. They issued the album in 1991 after the fall of the Berlin Wall. Somehow the album and its imagery perfectly overlapped the mood of those days. 18 million albums were sold and got the band a Grammy award.

That 'techno' curve run out of steam again. The 1997 *Pop* album disappointed and was one of their lowest selling albums. The *PopMart* tour to support the album left fans confused. They did not get the band's supposed joke on consumerism and modern art.[1] The band took another lease on life with *All That You Can't Leave Behind* in 2000. U2 went back to their roots, which is some kind of 'white soul'. 12 million copies changed hands. The album again managed to capture the spirit of the times. Following 9/11, people loved their positive message and music. That ability and courage to change is one of the reasons why the band survived for over 40 years.

3. Most only move when a crisis hits. However, it is hard to change in the middle of a mess. When the boat is sinking, all hands are needed to bail out water. It will absorb all your energy and most of management's time. It's hell. But it can be done.

Japan managed to do so in 1853. For several centuries, the country had chosen splendid isolation. Only a small trading station was eventually allowed to the Dutch on Deshima Island in Nagasaki harbour. The Dutch were tolerated because they were protestant and rated non-Christians. Christianity had in the 16th century made successful in-roads into Japan via Portuguese missionaries. Early in the 17th century, the religion was banned and ruthlessly supressed. Thousands were crucified. Foreigners were kicked out or killed. Contact with the outside world was restricted to the bare minimum. Consequently, by the mid 19th century, the land of the rising sun was still feudal. The country was carved into domains controlled by a daimyo. At the top of the hierarchy stood the Tokugawa shogun. The emperor was a mere figurehead. Daimyos had their own private samurai armies. The samurai figure has been much romanticised. Often however – just like medieval knights – they were ruthless, arrogant, violent men who could (and did) dispense justice based on a personal whim. Alien sailors who found themselves stranded on Japanese shores after a shipwreck were mercilessly eliminated. By the mid 1800s, European nations were fed up. They wanted those sailors to be protected and receive help. Also, they expected Japan to open for trade. To this end US President Millard Fillmore ordered Commodore Matthew Perry to Japan with a fleet of four warships.

Perry sailed into the Bay of Edo (now called Tokyo) on July 8, 1853. The shogun realized that the game was up. Japan could not compete with the military might of the West with samurai swords. There was no turning back, though it was attempted. After unsuccessful efforts to continue to keep the world out, the Meiji restoration of 1868 ended the shogunate. A program of radical reform was started. Japan caught up fast and shocked the world by annihilating the Russians in 1905. It was a milestone in military history: the defeat of a major European power by an Asian nation in an all-out war. Japan was back.[2]

The country had one major advantage: an existential crisis. That makes it easier to convince the organization that something must be done. To quote Sir Winston Churchill: 'Never let a good crisis go to waste.'

4. **An anticipatory or reactive approach towards change has one other benefit. It allows for an evolutionary approach. There is time. A crisis often demands a revolution. That incorporates far more risk and often a lot of upheaval.**

The French revolution was triggered by a severe credit crisis. It culminated in Robespierre's Reign of Terror (September 5, 1793–July 28, 1794) and years of chaos. Idem ditto for the Russian Revolution of 1917.

5. How does one know when the time is right to change?

Certainly, bad or weakening business results are an indication. Still, it's a hard question to answer because the future is inherently uncertain. Nobody can predict it. If truth sayers and paranormal mediums had any real skills, the CIA or Wall Street would recruit them and pay them fortunes. Here's what can be done:

a) *Take an active stance towards the future rather than simply accepting it as predetermined, and as leaders, take deliberate actions to shape it.*
b) Bob Johansen, Distinguished Fellow at the Institute for the Future, suggests that *'the best way to learn about the future is to immerse yourself in it'*. He believes the future is already here, just not broadly spread. Hence, we need to find the best way to experience and learn from that unevenly distributed future.[3]
c) *Be curious and listen.*[4] Earlier in this book, the need for an active network, for a 'Go and See' approach, and for a dedicated 'in-touch' program were highlighted.
d) *Constant testing and experimentation are essential.* Some tests will fail, some not, but all will provide new insights and vital learning.
e) *Forecasting in the strategy reviews.* Each review should include a reflection on possible futures and disruptions. Forecasting will not predict the future, but it will provoke thinking. Its role is to create insight and allow better strategic decisions in the present.
f) *Taking participations in new ventures.* This is a way to keep a finger on the pulse and to get understanding of what new business models could look like.

Let's talk how to change next.

EXECUTIVE SUMMARY:

1. Every business goes through cycles that take the shape of an S-curve. Ideally, one anticipates and creates a new growth curve when the business is still good, before the old model runs out of steam.//
2. The next best thing is a reactive response when the business is in stagnation.
3. Most only move when a crisis hits. That has the benefit of making the case of change easier but it's harder to do.
4. A proactive or reactive approach to change allows for an evolutionary approach. There is time. A crisis often demands a revolution. That incorporates far more risk and often a lot of upheaval.
5. Nobody can predict the future, but we can better manage it via (a) taking an active stand as leaders and proactively shape it. (b) Learn about the future by immersing ourselves in it. (c) Be curious and listen. (d) Constant testing and experimentation. (e) Forecasting in the strategy review. (f) Taking participations in new ventures.

C.
HOW TO CHANGE? WHAT IF THE LORD DOESN'T STRIKE YOU DOWN?

Saul of Tarsus was on the road to Damascus. He had a mandate issued by the High Priest to seek out and arrest followers of Jesus. His intent was to bring them back to Jerusalem for questioning and possibly execution. Suddenly he saw a blinding light (Acts 9). He fell to the ground and heard a voice say to him: 'Saul, Saul, why do you persecute me?' 'Who are you, Lord?' Saul asked. 'I am Jesus, whom you are persecuting,' the voice replied. 'Now get up and go into the city, and you will be told what you must do.'

Saul converted and became Saint Paul. *Such an epiphany is the first way that lasting change happens. However, we seldom experience it.*[1] It's hardly a good basis to run your business on. Of course, if you see the light (after reading this book for instance), do act on it.

Sometimes change happens via a radical switch in environment. An immigrant must often learn a new language and adopt new ways and beliefs. Employees from an acquired company are faced with the same reality. They too are immigrants in a way. It's quit or adapt. But again, these are not daily occurrences. ***What we need is a change management process***. Here are the vital components.

1. Get the organization to accept that change is needed.

'Hi, I'm John Doe, and I am an alcoholic'. Alcoholics Anonymous ('AA') start their sessions with this admission. AA is one of the most successful change programs ever devised. It has helped thousands of addicts to break the cycle. 22% of participants stayed sober for over 20 years. The very first step in their 12-step program is to accept that one is powerless over alcohol and that life has become unmanageable.

It's no different for any business. There must be an acknowledgment that things cannot go on as before, that the solutions that used to work won't work going forward, that a turning point has been reached. This recognition must be based on honest self-appraisal.

2. Convince the organization that they must act. Every change starts with a decision.

It's hard to achieve because organizations are generally averse to new ways. There are several reasons why this is the case:
a) <u>Vested interests</u>. A new approach may mean less power or prestige for certain people. Those at the top tend to like things to stay exactly as they are. It's good to be king. It took the revolution of 1789 and years of violence to break the supremacy of the aristocracy of the French Ancien Regime.

b) <u>Office politics</u>: promotion may hinge on maintaining the semblance that things are going well rather than on sincerity. Unpleasant truths – such as telling a CEO that his strategy is wrong – are exactly that: unpleasant. That's why the nerdy genius usually gets beaten by the mediocre slick.
c) <u>Unconvinced people</u>. Some stakeholders honestly believe that the change direction is not right. They may act to ensure it fails. Or that *you* fail if they see you as a competitor for a top job.
d) <u>The devil we know versus the devil we don't</u>. New ways are often uncertain. The organization tends to prefer what they are used to. It's a comfort zone.
e) <u>We are all creatures of habit</u>. Let's talk about these in detail in point 3.

If you are the one advocating significant change, get ready to take the punches. It's often said that leadership requires courage. That's true enough but it might not be an altogether pleasurable experience. Change is always difficult, especially when it comes to Go-to-Market Models that had as much prolonged success as the Gillette one. I was Vice President for Shave Care in CEEMEA. By 2008, it became clear that parts of the model had run their course. Historically, Gillette always focused on the top 'system' technology only. When a new one was introduced, the old one became 'legacy'. For instance, when Fusion came on the market in 2006, all marketing and innovation on Mach 3 was stopped. The idea was that Mach 3 users would trade up to the new, superior technology. Just as Sensor users had earlier gone to Mach 3, and before from other razors to Sensor.

Regretfully, CEEMEA consumers weren't trading up in sufficient numbers. They held on to Mach 3. One of the reasons was 'threshold performance'. Once a product has reached a certain level of performance, it gets harder to get people to upgrade. Mach 3 users did indeed already receive a very good shave. As these consumers were no longer advertised to, they started to drift away from the franchise. The image I used was that of a flock of sheep at a river crossing. Some had crossed (to Fusion land). Others had not and stayed behind (in Mach 3 land). These no longer received attention. What happened was that some animals were eaten by wolves, others drifted away, some fell in a crevasse. That's what was happening to our Mach 3 consumer base.

A new approach was suggested: to develop a portfolio approach, to advertise and innovate on Mach 3 as well, on the Blue 3 disposable, on top of Fusion. This met with resistance. Valid concerns were raised. The proposal was not the historical success model. A portfolio strategy was not proven at all. Would a portfolio not make cost skyrocket? R&D and media would now be needed on several streams. Consider also that Gillette was a recently acquired company. Hence, there was a feeling amongst some heritage Gillette executives of 'P&G'ers tinkering with a business they don't fully understand.' It was eventually agreed to do a test market in Russia. It worked. The portfolio approach became part of the new Go-to-Market Model.

3. Create new habits and find the keystone habit.

Habits are essential because they save energy. Brainpower is overwhelmingly costly. Conscious control is powerful, but it is draining, makes us feel tired, stressed, overwhelmed.[2] Imagine we had to question everything we do as soon as we get out of bed. It would drive us nuts. Instead, we rely on a routine. The brain stops participating in decision-making and can focus on other things. Habits don't require much bandwidth in the brain. Organizations and individuals alike are prisoners of habits. To break them is not easy, precisely because it requires effort. One must fight the habit.

To break habits, we must first understand them.[3] Let's talk about one of my bad habits. Come 3 o'clock, I go down to the company kitchen, I take a coffee and chocolate. It starts with one piece of Belgian Côte d'Or hazelnut chocolate and ends with half the big bar eaten. Out went all my good intentions to lose three kilos. As per figure 23 on the next page, all habits start with a Trigger (it's three o'clock). This acts as a cue. Then comes the Routine (go down to the kitchen and eat the snack). Finally, there is a Reward (that chocolate tastes divine!).[4] The interesting thing is that the first time round, the brain sends positive signals when the snack is eaten. But over time, the brain anticipates the joy of chocolate. It develops a craving for the reward. ***Cravings drive habits.*** That's why you really desire that cigarette or that big juicy hamburger with fries well before the act of smoking or eating.

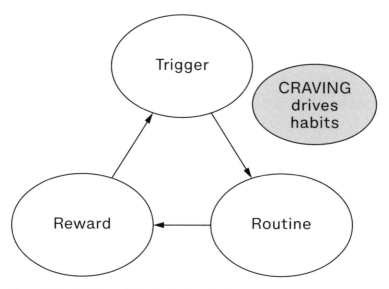

Figure 23: The Habit Loop (© Charles Duhigg, 'The Power of Habit')

The trick is to develop a new routine. Unless new routines are established, the habit pattern will unfold automatically.[5] An important question is to ask why. In my case: why do I snack? Is it because I'm hungry or because I'm a tad bored? If it is boredom, a changed routine could be to pick up my guitar for ten minutes instead of snacking. Perhaps a short walk in the garden. All of these would also give the right reward. If it is hunger that drives me, I could load the fridge with healthy snacks only and build a routine of raiding that larder. Some things help to break the habit:

a) Distance: remove temptation. In Flanders, we say: 'Don't put the cat with the milk.' If you'd like your organization to eat healthier, take away the soft drinks and the French fries.

b) Be public about the attempted change and create social pressure. If you want to get in shape with the goal of running the Antwerp ten miles, tell your friends about it. During the next dinner, they will inquire about how your preparation is going. It would be very annoying for your self-esteem were you to bail out. We all care about how others see us. If you want to reach a goal in your company, declare it.

c) <u>Join a community with good habits</u>. It's well established that 'smokers who live mostly among non-smokers tend to have higher rates of quitting, indicating again the power of social influence and social support.'[6] If you'd like your company to do better on sustainability, become part of the B-certified community for instance.

d) <u>Monitoring</u>. What gets measured, gets done. Any change program needs clear Key Performance Indicators ('KPIs') and these need to be followed up. For those embarking on a diet: write down what you eat. Step on the scales every morning.

e) <u>Find the keystone habit</u>. *A keystone habit starts a chain reaction. One change creates lots of other changes, it starts a process that transforms everything.* It's a lever that uplifts everything else. Consequently, some habits matter more than others. Keystone habits define company culture.

Alcoa Corporation is an American industrial corporation. It is the world's eighth largest producer of aluminum, with corporate headquarters in Pittsburgh, Pennsylvania. In 1987, the company had run into a rut. Investors were very dissatisfied and rejoiced when the board fired the CEO. The new CEO was Paul O'Neill. Most people at Wall Street had never heard of him. To remedy that, a meet and greet was set up. Every major investor was eager to take part in the event. Mr. O'Neill shocked the attendants. After his speech, Wall Street analysts ran out and started calling their investors with the urgent request to sell their stock in Alcoa. One said: 'The board put a crazy hippy in charge and he's going to kill the company.'

What happened was that O'Neill did not deliver the usual in his speech (more profits and lower cost, synergies, rightsizing…). Instead, he declared that he would focus on one keystone habit. He wanted to put all efforts on worker safety with the intention to make Alcoa the safest company in America. 'I want to go for zero injuries.' Was he right? Within a year, Alcoa's profits were record high. By the time O'Neill retired in 2000, market capitalization had risen by $27bn. Those who did not heed Wall Street's advice and held on to their stock would see the value rise fivefold. Just dividends paid back the original investment. Safety majorly improved. The worker injury rate fell to 5% of the U.S. average. Alcoa's CEO had understood the power of a keystone habit. Worker safety discipline created an overall culture of excellence.[7]

> At P&G Morocco, we implemented the rule of starting at 9 o'clock, of stricter entry routes at reception, of wearing the name badge and the no jeans policy. That discipline seeped through to all other areas.

f) <u>Start tiny.</u> BJ Fogg, founder of the behavior design lab at Stanford, has had major success with an approach where the habit change starts small, put where it fits naturally in someone's life and nurtured from there to growth. The Tiny Habits Method starts with small actions that can

be done in less than thirty seconds.[8] Its anatomy consists of three parts:
i. An anchor moment: This is an existing routine that reminds one of the new behavior.
ii. A tiny new behavior. It's done immediately after the anchor moment.
iii. Instant celebration, right after step ii.[9]

As an example, after brushing one's teeth, do two small push-ups. If you're unfit just do them via pushing yourself away from a wall. Tell yourself you did a good job afterwards.

There is veracity in the saying that from small things, big things come.

4. **Understand barriers and insights via the methodology used to develop successful advertising.**

What is the role of advertising? It is to change your behavior. Instead of buying Omo detergent, you are influenced to buy Tide. In just 30 seconds, this switch must be achieved. Analyzing the fundamental process that drives effective advertising is therefore valuable since business transformation initiatives often necessitate changes in organizational behavior as well. *The core premise is that people do something because they think something. If you want them to do something different, they must think something different.* As an example, if you thought President Trump will make America great again, your vote went to him. If you had a very different belief, you voted for President Biden. *However, in people's mind, there is usually a barrier.* These are defined as beliefs or feelings about your Brand's current strategic benefit that are in the minds of a sizeable set of consumers, that stand between what they currently do, and what you want them to do. Barriers are nearly always one of the four in the table below and they can be translated into what happens when a corporate change program is announced.

ADVERTISING	IN A CORPORATE CHANGE PROGRAM
I do not need the benefit: 'I do not need Tide's superior cleaning.'	'We do not need to change. We are making a lot of money as it is.'
I already have the benefit: 'Omo cleans just as well.'	'We are already doing plenty of change programs, there's no need to do more.'
I cannot afford the benefit: 'Tide is way too expensive for me.'	'I'll be out of a job if this change happens, it will lead to restructuring.'
I do not believe the benefit: 'There's no way Tide can get these stains out.'	'Really? This change program will make zero difference. It's just another management fad.'

Barriers can be tackled with an insight. This is a thought, feeling or piece of information which target consumers would accept, that helps them overcome their benefit barrier, and thus increases the relevance of the brand benefit. Insights can be around a product, value, or an emotion. While data analysis plays an important role in generating such insights, it also requires a certain level of artistry, honed through years of experience and emotional intelligence (EQ).

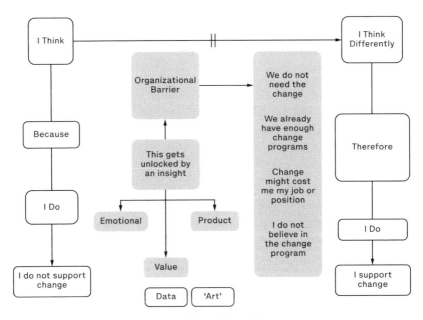

Figure 24: Barriers and Insights Applied to a Change Program

Let's review a couple of Marketing examples to illustrate the process. Vicks VapoRub is a cough and colds medicine. It's a mentholated topical ointment rubbed by hand on the neck and chest of the patient. Consumers however had an issue. They agreed that VapoRub was an effective remedy yet used other brands. They felt it was unpleasant to put their fingers in the slightly sticky, greasy texture of the product.

The insight that brought the business back was that care for a sick child requires more than giving a pill. It also requires parental love. VapoRub was successfully positioned as 'touch therapy', as an expression of parental care.

Folgers instant coffee advertised a richer taste. Consumers did not believe that. They argued that all instant coffees tasted the same. Therefore, they constantly switched brands. The insight was that freshly ground coffee served in top class restaurants represented the gold standard. If Folgers could reach that standard, consumers would believe its 'richer taste' claim. A wonderful 'hidden swap' campaign was developed. The coffee served in well-known restaurants was secretly replaced by Folgers Instant. People were then interviewed at their table on how they rated the coffee. They all agreed that it was excellent. 'Can I have another cup?' It was then revealed that the coffee was Folgers to astonished 'wows'.

Let's now see how to use this understanding of barriers and insights in stakeholder management.

5. Practice stakeholder mapping.

As one embarks on the change, it's important to spend time on understanding stakeholders as per the methodology below.

WHO	GOALS	RESOURCES	BARRIERS	INSIGHTS
Who is – and needs to be – involved in your change effort? 1. Champions 2. Opponents 3. Neutrals who might switch	What do they want? Is it aligned with your (change) goals? What do they think today and what should they think to make the change a success?	What resource do they have to help drive (or block) change? How to mobilize them?	What makes them less good at change? What barriers do they have that you need to help remove?	What will they do in the face of your change effort? What insights will you employ to get their support?

Figure 25: Stakeholder Mapping (Source: based on a model shared at CEDEP / INSEAD Business School)

If we apply this methodology to the P&G Morocco restructuring, champions would be management and employees in favor of change, mostly the best rated ones who were secure in their jobs. Still, we had to ensure that the executive level at the very top of P&G was fully briefed, agreed the approach and understood the risks. What if the Wall Street Journal would pick up on violent strikes in Morocco, so close to 9/11? What if the Moroccan King would pick up the phone and call the CEO? P&G's executive level's involvement was also important internally, especially in managing expectations and giving us time. The Morocco crisis was not something that could be fixed in a jiffy. We got full management support.

Towards employees it is essential to be clear about who stays and who goes in a restructuring (and in an acquisition) as soon as possible. This at least puts part of the organization in the neutral zone. 'Ouf, I still have a job.' The government would at best be neutral but if mismanaged could turn into an opponent because of promises made in the investment agreement. Or because restructurings in a difficult economic climate are never popular. Earlier, the approach towards the government was discussed. We also knew that the government wanted a positive restructuring case. This to combat the image that the labour law was difficult to handle in Morocco. We promised we'd do our best to deliver just such a case.

The Union would be an opponent, as were employees at risk of losing their job. The Union had significant resources to block the change. They could call a crippling strike or regular sit-downs. Legally, an agreement had to be reached with them. But there was no legal timeline. Negotiations could therefore drag on forever. How to avoid that? We introduced the concept of voluntary departure. Some employees with a lot of seniority could get a royal package based on historical precedent (anyway always the starting base for negotiations with unions). Those who accepted these terms pressured the Union to get an agreement ASAP. Therefore, they became avid champions. We also genuinely tried to come up with a win-win and outsourcing help for those employees who lost their jobs.

These are just some examples. Let me add a last one: ***mind the language***. We never called it a restructuring. It was a 'plan de modernisation', an effort to get the company ready for open borders and to ensure the viability of the local production centres in that brave new world. This was not cynicism. It was truthfully what we aimed to achieve.

6. Drive belief via early wins.

When do you have friends, queues of friends? When you win. It's a human trait. There's a delightful anecdote from early 19th century France about Napoleon's return to France when he escaped from his first exile in Elba (until he lost at Waterloo, 100 days later). It consists of headlines from the 'Moniteur Universel', the official French government-run newspaper, reporting on Napoleon's advance on Paris as follows:
March 10: the Corsican ogre has landed on Cape Juan.
March 12: the monster slept at Grenoble.

March 14: the usurper is directing his steps towards Dijon, but the brave and loyal Burgundians have risen 'en masse' and surrounded him on all sides.
March 19: Bonaparte is advancing with rapid steps, but he will never enter Paris.
March 20: Napoleon will, tomorrow, be under our ramparts.
March 21: The emperor is at Fontainebleau.
March 22: His Imperial Majesty, yesterday evening, arrived at the Tuileries, amidst the joyful acclamations of his devoted and faithful subjects.[10]

I must disappoint you: this story is both false and true. It was invented by another newspaper in 1815, to make fun of the next bunch of turncoats following Napoleon's final defeat. Yet, the story is totally true because it is how the world works. Winning puts the organization on your side. Proof is better than promises.

> **The P&G Morocco Challenge:**
>
> The barrier when the new OGSM was rolled out was that many employees did not believe it would work. They knew the crisis went deep. The challenge ahead did not seem like 'Mission Itspossible'. Sure, all applauded politely when the strategy was first discussed. But it's at the coffee machine where you see the real reactions, where people talk in hushed and confidential tones.
>
> Early wins were thus essential to show that the change was real and achievable, that we were on our way. Refurbishing was done everywhere to create a zero 'broken windows' environment. The sales force got new cars.

A high-profile training program ('Knowledge Miles') was started. People are convinced by facts, what they can see with their own eyes. Therefore, create them. You may run a Microbattle to get the data to support the change direction. What also helps is outsiders' support. Sometimes there is the lingering suspicion by the more sceptical part of the organization that management is merely putting up a smokescreen. Hence, the 'U.F.O. Maroc' program which exposed employees to external stakeholders. These would also talk about the challenges of open borders and the consequences of not acting.

Do celebrate early wins. Throw a party. It's very rewarding and motivational for the organization. **But speak the truth on the challenge ahead.** We minced no words when laying out the dire situation we were in. Neither did Sir Winston Churchill when the UK faced its darkest hour in WWII. When he met his Cabinet on May 13, 1940, he told them: 'I have nothing to offer but blood, tears and sweat.' That phrase was repeated later in the House of Commons. It's this level of honesty that helped rally the nation in their resistance to the Nazis. Sir Winston also said that there is 'no worse mistake in public leadership than to hold out false hopes soon to be swept away.'

A last word on Tide. Consumers did not believe that Tide had changed and now offered a superb performance. One anecdote to illustrate the situation: when we showed advertising on new Tide's cleaning performance in a focus group, some respondents said: 'Great ad for Omo'. This surprised us, didn't the commercial show Tide's packaging and logo? 'Ah no', came the response,

'Tide cannot do this. Hence, it should be an Omo ad.' The only way to convince house managers was to deliver real, tangible proof. We went street by street to introduce the new improved product, selling samples at very low cost, doing neighborhood road shows, asking shopkeepers to try the product so they could recommend it, taking back all the old Tide from shelves so no consumer would ever be disappointed again. Consumers had to experience the product themselves to believe in new Tide's cleaning performance and splendid suds profile.

7. **Define and frame the Mission accurately. Apply the 'Mission Success Equation' and 'F.A.Y.U.R.'.**

An essential question is: are the issues topical or structural? As an example, the HBR reported that 80% of all CEOs dislike or are unimpressed by their CMO.[11] For CFOs, this is not the case. For them, the equivalent number is only 10%. The C-suite function with the lowest tenure is the CMO role (4.1 years versus 8 years for a CEO). CMOs only seldom make it to CEO. It cannot be that nearly every CMO cannot be trusted or is talentless. This indicates a structural issue in the job definition. One is that CMOs are tasked to be strategic but are often marginalized on decision rights. Moreover, there is a prejudice towards 'creative profiles'. One McKinsey partner admitted that CEOs and CFOs see CMOs as 'replaceable divas'.

In Morocco, we had to change just about everything. The trouble was that resources did not allow us to tackle everything at once. That's usually the case. Choices had to be made. It simply could not be that 90% of employees did not know how to make a quality product or good advertising anymore. The issue was structural. That was the key driver behind the priority setting in the change program. We had to break the 'Moroccan Paradox' via structurally improving the cost structure and rightsizing the organization. The 'plan de modernisation' (yes that included the executive team) was a must-do, ASAP. Launch the quality improvement plan via the 'ISO-X' 6 Sigma program (discussed earlier). Bad quality does lead to higher cost. Structurally fix Tide's quality across the entire value chain and marketing mix. Certainly, a lot more had to be – and was – done. Yes, some of the advertising was not good enough, but it was not a fundamental issue. It was only a topical matter.

The Meiji Restoration in Japan was faced with the same challenge as P&G Morocco. They had to move from a feudal world to the modern world in the shortest possible time. Everything had to change. Focus was put on three areas (do note how 'integrated' the approach was):
a) Reform the military.
b) Military might was essential to get out of 'unequal treaties'. These were forced on the Japanese by the West and had majorly hurt local pride. One of the clauses said that foreigners could not be judged in Japanese courts of law but only by their own laws and tribunals, even when the crime was committed in Japan.
c) Set up a modern tax system to afford the military revolution.[12]

There's one more lesson to be drawn from this historical event: *clad the new in the language of the old. This makes change easier to accept*. Things like: 'a return to the glory days of the company when we used to focus on these type of strategies' or 'back to our time-honored traditions' (in the case of Japan).

8. Know what to keep and pace the change.

Durk Jager took over as CEO of P&G in September 1999. Mr. Jager came in with a great track record having earlier successfully managed Japan and the USA. He was the first non-American CEO and had all the candidness so characteristic of the Dutch. He was a man with fresh, bold ideas and the courage to implement them. He set out to reshape P&G. The company had a stodgy corporate culture and had not created any exciting new brand in years. Just 17 months later he was ousted. The P&G stock price had crashed after missing the forecast again and a botched acquisition. What went wrong? 'We took on too much change too fast', declared John E. Pepper, a retired CEO, who was reinstalled as Chairman. 'We clearly took on more than we were able to execute.'[13] A CEO from another company put it as: 'He knew what to change but not what to keep.' Some of the changes proposed were vital and important and were arguably overdue. But not everything had to change. It was chaotic. A.G. Lafley came in as the next CEO and refocused the effort (keeping elements of Jager's agenda actually). The business and organization recovered.

I later read that Jack Welch regretted that he had only been able to deliver his change agenda over 20 years at G.E. My first reflection was that if had he tried to do it in two years, he'd have gone the way of Durk Jager. Amazon's founder Jeff Bezos noted that he was always asked the question: 'What is going to change in the future?' But he is rarely asked: 'What is not going to change?' Mr. Bezos believes that the second question is more important than the first 'because you can build strategy around it.'[14]

Back to the Meiji Restoration in Japan. The decision was wisely made to keep some things. The Japanese script remained, though it is more complex than the Latin script. The emperor's status was restored. Moral of the story: any organization can only take so much change. 'Change fatigue' will set in. Therefore, make sure to focus the effort on what truly matters.

> *Pace the effort. Decide on what not to do or only at a later stage.* As mentioned in the Morocco case, P&G owned the distributor company, 'Comunivers'. This was not the best solution going forward. It was too expensive. P&G's way of doing business in emerging markets is to outsource part of the distribution. We decided that it would create too much disruption to do the 'plan de modernisation' and at the same time completely overhaul the distribution. Also, there was no ready alternative available in the local market at the time. Eventually, Comunivers was outsourced but five years later.

Tony Saldanha, who's an expert on digital transformations, also calls out the risk of trying to do too much in one go. He identifies it as one of the key reasons why such transformations fail. He recommends to de-risk a major transformation. 'Chunking the work into smaller iterative deliveries and constant learning' is key to avoid big, embarrassing failures.[15]

9. Empower a guiding coalition.

John P. Kotter sees this as an essential part of the process. In his influential HBR Article, *Leading Change*, Mr. Kotter suggests giving the leadership to a group with shared commitment and enough power.[16] It's not right to relegate team leadership to HR or a staff member. It's best to put a senior line manager in charge. One can also decide to have this team work outside of the normal hierarchy. ***People who recommend the change should be the ones who must live with it.*** It's too easy to make recommendations that others are told to execute later. It's also a good learning process for those involved. They will experience first-hand what worked and what did not.

10. Those not willing to get on the bus must leave.

In his study on how companies can get from *Good to Great*, Jim Collins calls out the need to first decide on 'who' and only then on 'what'.[17] He convincingly uses the image of a bus. Before heading off towards the new destination, get the right people on the bus first. Rationale:

a) If one begins with the 'who' rather than the 'what', it's easier to adapt to a changing world. If people only join because of the direction, and the direction changes, it creates problems.

b) The people who willingly step on the change bus are easier to motivate and/or are more self-motivated.

c) If you have the wrong people, you simply cannot get to the destination. Sometimes, you just have the wrong crew.

We used that image of the bus when presenting the change program in Morocco. Employees were told that it would be a very rocky journey. If that was not for them, it was time to leave. They were asked for a decision: either on the bus or not. We hoped they'd join. If they did, we promised that the experience would be one of the most exciting business adventures they'd ever have in their careers. They would learn a ton. 99% signed up for the ride of a lifetime.

11. **Don't underestimate emotion and psychology. EQ matters.**

P&G bought Gillette in 2005. Gillette employees were less than thrilled by the event. I oversaw the integration for CEEMEA. The new employees could not stop romancing about how much better life in Gillette had been (I do agree that it was a great company. That's why $57bn was paid for it). They certainly employed nicer titles. The question was raised in the integration team whether we should force the P&G titles on the Gillette heritage employees. We vetoed it. Do people care about titles? They do, passionately so. What is the cost of calling somebody 'executive manager' instead of 'manager'? Zero. So, what did it matter what they put on their business cards? But the emotional loss of taking the title away was significant, at a point where we were eager to retain as many well-rated Gillette employees as we could.

There was only one exception. If a Gillette employee moved into a traditional P&G division, they would have to accept the P&G title. That was an easy sell because many believed that such an assignment would be a plus in their future P&G

career. Now here's the magic: the psychology changed over time. What may not work at some point, may at a later stage. Right after the acquisition was announced the first reflex amongst Gillette employees was: 'Do I have a job?' Once that was clear, it turned to: 'Do I have a career?' And then it became: 'I am as much a P&G employee as somebody who started straight from university in the company.' After less than a year, those who came from Gillette insisted on the P&G titles. They wanted to fully belong and not be seen as different, as 'outsiders'. For instance, Gillette was initially housed in an office slightly separated from the main P&G office in Geneva. Gillette employees lobbied to move into the main building. That kind of evolution of the emotions occurs during any change program. Be aware of it and adapt as required.

12. Overcommunicate.

Change brings uncertainty and higher levels of stress. At those times, the leader must overcommunicate in a candid but confident way in town halls, videos, and business updates.

13. Effective change may require making people changes.

Levi's was in trouble. Net revenue had declined by 32% from a peak of $6.8bn to stagnate at $4.8bn for years. In 2011, Chip Bergh took over as CEO and completely revitalized the iconic apparel firm. He implemented an excellent new strategy. What he also did was remove or change nine out of ten senior managers. Sometimes the only way to transform a culture is to change the people.

I've mentioned that some CEOs were fired during their careers. Often, they then did exceptionally well in another assignment. The reason is related to context and culture. If you are a heavy metal guitarist and join a reggae company, you are in for a tough time. Even if the company claims they want to become headbangers, and you play as well as Eddie Van Halen. As soon as you turn the amp on, and start shredding, the organization will hate it. 'Too loud, this is not how we play, ridiculous stage act, this CEO does not understand us, no talent whatsoever, let's complain to the Board.' The only way to go metal will be to replace the players. Get it in writing from the Board that you have the authority to do so before accepting a change of job. If the Board insists on protecting the existing team, you are doomed. Let's take a page from history: kings and queens always changed their household upon accession and got rid of the previous court. As do US Presidents to this day.

EXECUTIVE SUMMARY:

1. Get the organization to accept that change is needed.

2. Convince the organization that they must act. Every change starts with a decision.

3. Create new habits and find the keystone habit. A keystone habit starts a chain reaction. One change creates lots of other changes, it starts a process that transforms everything. It's a lever that uplifts everything else. Consequently, some habits matter more than others. Keystone habits define company culture.

4. Understand barriers and insights via the methodology used to develop successful advertising.

5. Practice stakeholder mapping.

6. Provide real proof via early wins.

7. Define and frame the Mission. Apply the 'Mission Success Equation' and 'F.A.Y.U.R.'

8. Know what to keep and pace the change.

9. Empower a guiding coalition.

10. Those not willing to get on the bus must leave.

11. Don't underestimate emotion and psychology. EQ matters.

12. Overcommunicate.

13. Effective change may require making people changes.

PILLAR 4

CREATE A SUPER-CHARGED TEAM

Obviously, all concepts and tools introduced so far will go a long way towards motivating your team. Here are some other important areas to consider:

1. **Focus on culture, not just on more procedures and rules. Create the right one for your team and company.**

   > The P&G Morocco Challenge: The internal control issues during the crisis were a symptom of the general lack of executional excellence. Adding more procedures was not the solution because we already had a cupboard full of paper. The way to deal with it was to create the right culture.

   ≡ Culture is 'the way things are done around here'. It is what people do even when they are not asked to do it.

   Mr. Peter Drucker famously said that 'culture eats strategy for breakfast'. Don't get me wrong, there must be rules and procedures in several areas. It's just that by themselves these are not enough. Culture ensures that they are followed and absorbed, without the use of force and supervision. It must be 'in the blood' so to speak.

   Six key components to drive a culture deserve a deeper discussion: (a) tone from the top, (b) the reward system, (c) keystone habits, (d) rituals, (e) intrinsic motivation, and (f) the context.

a) <u>The tone from the top: leadership by example defines culture:</u>

Alexander the Great (356–323 BC) was an extraordinary leader. He drove his Macedonian phalanx on a victorious 10,000 miles march. But once arrived at the Indus, his soldiers would go no further (very much to the displeasure of their leader who sulked in his tent for three days before accepting the inevitable). Alexander then made the biggest mistake of his career. He took the way back through one of the most inhospitable places on earth, the coastal area of Baluchistan. The later explorers of this Makran desert 'suffered so bitterly that they could not believe Alexander went before them unless the place had been nicer to him than to them'.[1] It had not been. Of the 40,000 who followed Alexander, merely 15,000 survived this march through utter hell. At a desperate time like this, Alexander demonstrated what tone from the top is. In the words of his biographer, Arrian:

> *'The army was crossing a desert of sand; the sun was already blazing down upon them, but they were struggling on under the necessity of reaching water, which was still far away. Alexander, like everyone else, was tormented by thirst, but he was none the less marching on foot at the head of his men. It was all he could do to keep going, but he did so, and the result (as always) was that the men were the better able to endure their misery when they saw that it was equally shared. As they toiled on, a party of light infantry which had gone looking for water found some – just a wretched little trickle in a shallow gully. They scooped up with difficulty what they could and hurried back, with their priceless treasure to Alexander; then, just before they*

reached him, they tipped the water into a helmet and gave it to him. Alexander, with a word of thanks for the gift, took the helmet and, in full view of the troops, poured the water on the ground. So extraordinary was the effect of this action that the water wasted by Alexander was as good as a drink for every man in the army. I cannot praise this act too highly; it was a proof, if anything was, not only of his power of endurance, but also his genius for leadership.'[2]

Another ancient source, Chang Yü, a commentator from the Sung dynasty (960–1279 AD) on Sun Tzu wrote:

'…the general must be the first in the toils and fatigues of the army. In the heat of the summer, he does not spread his parasol nor in the cold of winter don thick clothing. In dangerous places he must dismount and walk. He waits until the army's wells have been dug and only then drinks; until the army's food is cooked before he eats; until the army's fortifications have been completed, to shelter himself.'[3]

It does not always need to be done via heroic acts. You can show an example in simple ways. I had the habit of always sending a handwritten birthday card to each member of the leadership team. Paul Polman sent ten cards every day to express gratitude to an employee. 'If you care about others, they'll care about you.'[4] In the end, there's no secret. If you want loyalty in the company culture, show loyalty; not just upwards but also downwards. If you want a more disciplined organization, demonstrate discipline. It sets a tone. Galatians 6: 'A man reaps what he sows.'

Chip Bergh also told me that, even though people do not have access to the CEO's calendar, they quickly figure out where and on what time is spent. 'If you are often in stores and close to the market, that is visible and becomes part of the culture.'

b) The reward system:

People are smart, they figure it out. Quickly, they get a feel for where the boundaries are. Much as the organization tells you that they absolutely love the company purpose, they are also driven by personal selfish goals. They need to make money and have ambition. If the CEO declares that, as of tomorrow, those who wear pink double the chances of promotion and a hefty bonus, what will the color of the season be? Equally, if it's declared that brown shoes are out and will delay promotions, we'll see less of that hue.

The reward system has to tie in completely with the strategic goals and the culture one wants to create. One multinational in the late 90s in Western Europe decided to reward countries for revenue growth. Profit responsibility however was at the regional level, not the country level. If you are a country manager only evaluated and rewarded for the top-line, why care about cost control and the bottom-line? On the contrary, it is best to spend as much as possible to drive top-line revenue. Predictably, the result was a profit massacre.

Rewards can indeed have unintended consequences on behavior. Gustav Heinrich Ralph von Koenigswald (1902–982) was a paleontologist and geologist who conducted research on hominins, including *Homo erectus*. Whilst working and digging in Java, he offered the locals money for every fragment of skull they would provide. As a result, every time somebody found an intact skull, they'd smash it to be able to cash in piece by piece.[5] Von Koenigswald would then spend ages to put the puzzle together.

> Rewards do not always have to be massive. They can be small tokens of public appreciation. It's especially good to reward the 'doers' and the 'lower' ranks. At P&G Morocco, every month we'd have Flower Power and Hot Chocolate. Everybody could recommend somebody who in their opinion deserved this reward. Nominated female employees were given 21 roses. Males received boxes of Belgian Godiva chocolates. Cost? Negligible. Impact? Major. I have yet to meet the first employee who gets praised in public with a nice bouquet and is unhappy about it.[*]

Robert A. McDonald had the same experience. 'Awards, trophies, a signed picture, it may sound tacky, but it works.'[6] Mr. McDonald adds that when recognizing people with tokens of appreciation, one is trying to create a culture of appreciation – 'grateful people are happy people' – and an environment where effort is rewarded. It is not simply manipulating the people with bogus awards. What are medals in the end? Just bits of metal and some cloth. Except that is not what they are. They carry tremendous meaning in their respective cultures. They represent honor, courage, and heroism and what we believe is best about us.

---

[*] Those who were not rewarded may be unhappy about it. 'Why them and not me?'. Two points on that: have a transparent and fair process on how awards are granted and then don't care about the whining. Because if you have to keep everybody happy all the time, you'll end up doing nothing.

An important tool to drive culture resides in the promotion policy. It is a universal human trait to favor people whose styles and career paths resemble our own. That is fine if one wants to continue with the dominant corporate culture. However, if the strategy asks for new skills (see Capabilities chapter 9), different behaviors and culture, then it logically follows that different people need to be promoted to key positions. We'll end on a great Navy SEALs saying: *'It's not what you preach, it's what you tolerate'*. The suggestion that praise is best done in public and chastising in private is valid. There's one important caveat. If negative feedback was meted out behind closed doors, one must still let the organization know that corrective action was taken. If not, they do not know that you acted and will assume that you were tolerant of the misbehavior. Employees will start to think: 'If he or she can do this, why not me? If that person can show up at 10.30 in the morning, why do I have to drag myself out of bed to be on time?' Before you know it, half the people are late.

c) <u>Find the keystone habit</u>:

All habits are not created equal. Some are keystone habits. These have a chain effect on other behaviors. Company culture is shaped by keystone habits. These were covered in the Change Management section.

d) <u>Rituals</u>:

Before each karate lesson, every student must perform a salute. The group stands in one row according to seniority, from black belt to white belt. We face the 'sensei' (teacher) and a picture of Gichin Funakoshi, the founder of modern karate.

After kneeling, eyes are closed for a moment of reflection, then there's a bow to the sensei and to the shomen ('the front of the dojo'). Oss! One could berate it as archaic mumbo jumbo. Because should self-defense ever be needed, one can hardly tell the attacker: 'Erm Sir, excuse me, but I need to bow first.' Yet, the salute has a very important function in training. It means 'I'm entering a different world, the world of the dojo. Yes, I have issues with my boss, bills to pay and my partner wants to kill me, but for the duration of the training, this chapter is closed in my mind, and I will focus on my training.' That focus is essential because as of black belt, all training is highly realistic. Attacks are 'skin touch'. It takes but a couple of centimetres for skin touch to become a serious injury. At the end of the session, one returns to the world via a short salute.

All religions, cultures, all elite organizations thrive on rituals. They create a sense of belonging and identity. They make us feel like we belong to a continuum (e.g. West Point: 'the long gray line'), to something that is bigger than ourselves. Families benefit from rituals too: driving home for Xmas, the Thanksgiving meal, Iftar at the end of a day of Ramadan fasting, and so on. Sometimes new rituals need to be created. Gillette was an acquired company for P&G in 2005. Integrations are never easy for the 'acquired' employees. As the saying goes: 'It's better to buy than to be bought'. As Gillette and P&G heritage employees were mixed in CEEMEA, it was important to recreate an esprit de corps. Amongst others, we introduced a club tie and a silk scarf. What was great about it was that the new portfolio strategy was reflected in the green/orange/blue striped tie and scarf design. Though business casual was the new norm, we'd all wear suits and the club tie in important meetings. We were Gillette, the best a man can get. We called ourselves the 'Rock Hard Team'. At one point, the team won a lot of internal awards. At the ceremony, when Gillette team members came forward to collect their award, the audience refused to clap. They did something far better. Spontaneously, the whole room stamped their feet and clapped their hands in the 'boom boom tjak' rhythm of Queen's 'We Will Rock You' anthem. Experiences like that create cohesion, a unique team spirit.

Interestingly, shaving in the morning is a ritual as well. It means 'getting ready for battle'. No man goes back to bed after shaving (not unless there is a good reason anyway).

e) <u>Intrinsic motivation</u>:

People have three innate psychological needs: autonomy, mastery and relatedness to a purpose.[7] Autonomy is the desire to lead our own lives. Mastery is the joy we take from being great at something, or to get better at it. Purpose is the feeling of belonging to a greater cause than ourselves. These drive motivation without control, direction, or extra salary. Anything that can be done on these areas helps create culture.

It must be highlighted though that, once again, the context must be considered. When on the Titanic – P&G Morocco for instance was a sinking ship – one is inevitably more directive and controlling. It's pump or drown. It also depends on the skill level of the organization. Are they all very junior or veterans of many wars? In other words, situational leadership is required.

f) Manage the context:

The power of context was covered before. Here's a last example to drive the point home: Volvo once did a study to understand why nice people can become monsters behind the steering wheel of a car. One reason is isolation. In public, nobody can yell 'dirty bastard' at somebody without censure and loss of reputation. But in the isolation of the car space, these inhibitions disappear.

2. Respect 'the diversity of the mind' of mavericks.

In chapter 7, we reviewed the Battle of Waterloo and how the failure of the French to take Quatre Bras proved of pivotal importance. When Marshall Ney's first troops arrived at the crossroads, they found it already occupied by the Allies. It was only so because of a maverick, Major-General Baron Jean Victor Constant de Rebecque. He had received orders from Wellington to move his Corps to a place which he was convinced was the wrong area. General Rebecque understood the critical importance of Quatre Bras and sent 4000 men there.[8] That act put a decisive clog in Napoleon's campaign.

Mavericks tend to get bad press. However, they are an essential element because they challenge conventional wisdom. Such challenges should be taken seriously. Use them as a test for the robustness of a plan. It's a misconception that those who disagree with a certain business strategy do so because they are difficult, 'immature' or non-believers. They challenge because they passionately believe there is another way (the caveat here is that discussions should take place at the time the plan is made. Once a decision is reached, all should focus on implementing the agreed plan).

Mavericks often have original ideas. In June 1941, 25-year-old Lieutenant Archibald David Stirling was lying in the Cairo hospital. He was paralyzed from the waist down following a botched - and frankly irresponsible - parachute jump. That character trait had already been noted in the assessment at the end of his officer training: 'irresponsible and unremarkable'. Stirling was considered so lazy he earned the moniker 'the Giant Sloth', no mean feat in an army. He lacked basic discipline, spent most of his time in bars and clubs, gambling and drinking.

Earlier in life he had miserably failed at every occupation tried (as a student thrown out of Cambridge for misbehavior, failed architect, mountain-climber, artist, officer). His last job was as a cowboy in the USA until his mother sent him a telegram informing him that war had broken out. He rejoined the Scots Guards regiment he had been in before, and was just as bored and undisciplined as ever. At a bar of an exclusive London gentleman's club, White's, Stirling heard about a new form of soldiering that he felt was a better personality fit. He signed up for a crack new commando unit, 'Layforce'. By 1941, Layforce was stationed in Egypt. They had gotten hold of some parachutes and decided to do the world's first desert parachute jump. Without the nuisance of preparatory training, Stirling and five others climbed into a Vickers Valentia. The plane was used to deliver mail and totally unsuitable for parachuting. The static line (which pulls open the chute as the paratrooper falls) was attached to the passenger seats. Lieutenant's Stirling went down way too fast. His parachute was badly ripped by the tailfin of the plane. Touchdown almost killed him. As he lay in hospital, he had lots of time to think. He thought up a revolutionary idea.

Stirling felt the British commando concept was not working. So far, they were used in too large and cumbersome units. The troops were therefore easily spotted and lost all elements of surprise. On top, they attacked the Axis forces stationed on the North African coast from the seaside. That's exactly where the Germans and Italians were expecting them. As a result, the commando attack results had been disappointing and British casualties high. But what if commandos begun their assualt from the opposite direction? The desert side was vast and considered impassable. It was unpatrolled and largely unprotected. A commando force of several hundred could only attack one target at a time. But what if one created lots of small units, that moved quickly, raided lightning fast in the rear of the enemy, retreating just as fast having placed timebombs, and destroyed several targets simultaneously?

Following some gutsy moves, and against strong resistance, Stirling eventually managed to sell his idea to the top brass. Sir Winston Churchill – another maverick–- loved the whole thing as a perfect example of British pluck and derringdo and provided his full support. Stirling's idea led to the creation of the SAS, the Special Air Service, Britain's elite Special Forces. The force was – and is – used to lethal results. It is the regiment on which SEALs, Delta Force and all modern special forces are modeled. Only somebody as unconventional as David Stirling could have thought it up and pulled it off.*[9]

Mavericks bring a unique perspective and diversity of thought, which is the most significant contribution of diversity. Neurologist Oliver Sachs claimed that the brains of an accountant use different circuitry versus that of a musician. That's the power of diversity: a fount of new and innovative ideas imagined by different brains that a non-diverse group could not have thought of. Note that I do not advocate to only employ 'square pegs for a round hole'. Key is to have different profiles. In setting up the SAS, David Stirling received vital support from his comrade in arms, Lieutenant John Steele Lewes. Lewes was his exact opposite: a man of military virtue, discipline, and a degree of personal austerity that many found insufferable. The point is that having both made the difference.

It's in a crisis that maverick thinking can be at its most useful. I've picked up a great story in this respect in a keynote by Ogilvy Vice Chairman Rory Sutherland. When bees find good flowers, they return to the hive and do a waggle dance. This dance communicates that a source of nectar has been found and it provides directions. But there are always some maverick bees who refuse to listen, and these go off in other directions. These misfits should be fired! Yet, they serve a vital role because they are the ones who find new sources of nectar. It's claimed that without these mavericks, the hive might die out. Also, the less food there is, the more bees become mavericks.

---

* Sadly, all too often John Maynard Keynes is proven right. 'Worldly wisdom teaches that it is better for reputation to fail conventionally than to succeed unconventionally'

Make maverick thinking part of the process, do not expect it just from an individual's courage. If you are the challenger on three consecutive occasions in an executive meeting, your image risks becoming that of a 'nay-sayer' – or that kiss of death – 'a rebel'. Pretty soon, people will prefer not to invite you. As Harvard Business School professor Amy Edmondson put it: 'Nobody ever got fired for silence'.[10] People know this all too well, which is why challenge must be made part of the process. That way, it's not a specific individual who has to stick his or her neck out. A good example is the Israeli 'tenth man' approach. When an important decision must be made, the tenth person must take the opposite position of the majority. Not because of a personal conviction but to make sure every decision is fully thought through. Another way is to run the aforementioned 'pre-mortem'. Before launch, one asks the question: 'Imagine our plan did not work. Why not?' Perhaps competition cut price much more aggressively than thought. Maybe the distribution build-up was a lot slower than what was promised. Corrective action can then be taken. Or one can hire two consultants when contemplating a deal. One consultant gets paid if you do the deal, the other if you don't.

Setting up an independent Red Team is also a good tool to get alternative thinking reflected. In the words of Micah Zenko: 'Red teaming is a structured process that seeks to better understand the interests, intentions, and capabilities of an institution – or a potential competitor – through simulations, vulnerability probes and alternative analyses.'[11] Israel uses Red Teams to find weaknesses with respect to terror attacks. One example: they investigated how long it would take to 3D print and copy a container seal (about ten minutes).

So, a terror organization could quickly place something on a ship, and nobody would notice it because the seal is intact.

3. Management by walking around.

This sounds like a joke out of a Dilbert cartoon but it's highly effective. It's essential for a leader to be visible. Walk around the office regularly and talk to all ranks. It's easy to find a subject to talk about; just look at what's up on the person's cubicle wall. Nobody puts their failures up. Au contraire. It's pictures of pride that are shown: a child's graduation from university, a wedding picture, a postcard from a trip, a family gathering. It also allows you to get to know employees as individuals. Ilham Kadri, CEO of Solvay, rightly stressed that it is good to remind ourselves that employees choose to work in the company, to be aligned and excited (or not) by the mission. They are in control.

4. Add some rock & roll.

Another rocket test does not sound like a terribly exciting event. Yet, SpaceX' 'Heavy Falcon' launch was followed on TV by an enthusiastic crowd. Every key step was filmed, from countdown to the gracious landing of the reusable boosters. Since it was a test, and the whole thing could go up in flames at lift-off, no expensive satellite was added. Instead, Elon Musk's red Tesla Roadster was added as a dummy payload. A mannequin in a spacesuit, nicknamed Starman, was put in the driver's seat with his arm casually hanging out, as if on a laid-back California summer outing. Loud cheers went up in sports bars when the payload was successfully released. At that precise moment David Bowie's *Life on Mars?* played.

The screen in the car displayed the words 'don't panic', a reference to Douglas Adams' classic *The Hitchhiker's Guide to the Galaxy*. As a result of these creative touches, the launch was a tremendously engaging event.[12]

Let's do something like that for our company initiatives as well. We spend so much time in the office that we might as well enjoy it. It does not have to be rocket science. Bringing an ice-cream cart or Belgian waffles when a key project is successful does the trick as well.

> **EXECUTIVE SUMMARY:**
>
> 1. Create the right culture via the six key components: (a) tone from the top, (b) the reward system, (c) keystone habits, (d) rituals, (e) intrinsic motivation, and (f) the context.
> 2. Respect the diversity of the mind of mavericks.
> 3. Manage by walking around.
> 4. Add some rock & roll.

*PULLING IT ALL TOGETHER
IN ONE MODEL:*

THE LEAN ORGANISM MANAGEMENT MODEL

Let's investigate how everything fits together in the Lean Organism Management Model (back to figure 2). This is an integrated management system, from the executive top, down to every single employee. It ensures that everybody works towards achieving the strategic objective. It's an organism, not unlike the human body. It is a unified whole in which the parts work in relation with each other. To continue the body metaphor, it also means one cannot cut bits and pieces out of it and hope to function just as well.

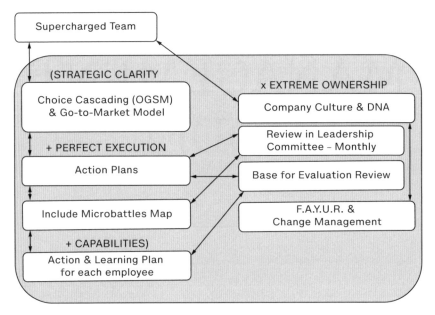

Figure 2: The Lean Organism Management Model™
(© 2017 Peter Corijn / VUCASTAR)

The executive leadership delivers the Strategic Clarity via the OGSM and Go-to-Market Model. Below, there is no need for further strategy documents but for Action Plans by each department. Admittedly, companies of a large size and/or with very different business lines need another layer of business specific OGSMs that must link into the overall strategy.

However, the bias should be to get into action and Perfect Execution. The Action Plan describes how the strategy will be delivered, as per figure 26. It cascades the strategy down to each department and each single employee. On top, there is a Microbattle Map (see Capabilities, chapters 9 and 2) with tests around must-win battles. Every employee also has a learning plan (see Capabilities, chapters 9 and 5).

STRATEGY	ACTION	KPIs	WHO / WHEN	STATUS	REVIEW
As per OGSM	2 to max 3 key actions for each strategy	Clear mesures	Account-ability	2 to 3 bullet points	RED / AMBER / GREEN Only 'reds' get discussed Monthly review in Business Committee 'Action Room' (put as A3 on wall of meeting room)

Figure 26: The Action Plan (© 2017 Peter Corijn / VUCASTAR)

These plans get reviewed every month in the Executive Meeting. I like to put A3 copies on the wall to create an Action Room. The status of each action must be coded red/amber/green. Each department in turn reviews how they are doing. The leader of each department does not have the right to delegate the presentation. They ought to know their numbers and be fully up to date, including all the particulars. None of the 'let me call somebody who knows' stuff. Senior executives must display No Excuse Ownership. The Action Room is one of the critical points where the CEO gets involved in the execution of strategy.

Ford CEO Alan Mulally insisted on this kind of discipline when he saved the company from a meltdown. In 2008, the prospects were bleak. General Motors and Chrysler were bailed out by Congress, but Ford saved itself.[1] Only the 'red' coded activities get discussed. This must be done in a spirit of collaboration. The objective is to seek advice and support: 'How can we help you to get back on track?' Well, maybe more marketing support is needed. Or we underestimated the competitive reaction and will need to increase our digital spending. Can this be funded?

Action Plans are the base for the yearly performance and bonus review, which further drives ownership. Action Plans get cascaded down to each individual employee.

The company has ideally also implemented F.A.Y.U.R. and mastered Change Management Skills. These must be part of the company's culture, ways of working and DNA. All elements reinforce and feed into each other. They create and are simultaneously driven by a Supercharged Team in a virtuous cycle.

This chapter concludes 'True Leaders Deliver'. I'd like to end with something from P&G Morocco, the case we've discussed in depth. Here's one of the posters used in the office.

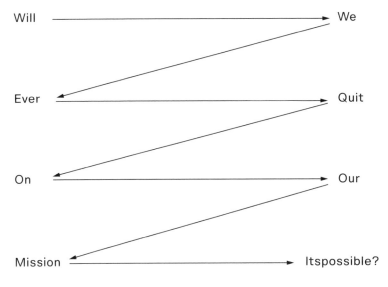

(Your head movement gave you the answer)

We never quit and delivered the Mission. Good luck on yours!

EXECUTIVE SUMMARY:

1. The Lean Organism is an integrated, total system, from the executive top, down to every single employee. It ensures that everybody works towards achieving the strategic objective.
2. The bias should be to get into Action Plans. The action plan describes how the strategy will be delivered.

ACKNOWLEDGMENTS

Lots of what I share has come from the thinking and experience of others. To paraphrase Newton, I merely stand on the shoulders of giants. I've given credit where credit is due. If I have inadvertently omitted the accurate reference, please inform the publisher and we will make the necessary corrections in future print runs.

Many executives and others devoted precious time to share their wisdom on various topics. I want to thank them again for their generosity. Ms. Alison Cooper, Messrs. Nigel Boardman, Koen Bouuaert, Chip Bergh, Denis Christiaens, Jef Colruyt, Dixie Dansercour, Tom Dechaene, Philiep Dedrijvere, Sanjay Dhiri, David Haines, Marc Herremans, Praga Khan, Robert A. McDonald, Peter Mead, Paul Polman, Kevin Roberts, Andrew Robertson, Sir Martin Sorrell, Rory Sutherland, Colonel Sharon Gat, (Ret.) SEALs Rob Robertson and John 'Sully' Sullivan all agreed to be interviewed. Ms. Sophie Blum arranged my visit to the Israeli Airforce. Claude Meyer and Yves Debruyne were kind enough to review the manuscript. Tony Saldanha provided support in getting my book proposal to agents and publishers. Thomas Barta gave further insight on the publishing business. Thanks also to all those who were kind enough to provide endorsements. I apologize if I have missed somebody.

ACKNOWLEDGMENTS

My spouse Saskia deserves profound gratitude for her relentless editing. Additionally, special thanks to Ms. Sophie Vanluchene, Ms. Nina Waegemans, and everybody at Borgerhoff & Lamberigts (Owl Press) for believing in this book. Your comments and insights were priceless.

Every success mentioned was achieved due to the talent and commitment of a great team. Mistakes are my own.

Peter Corijn
Flanders, Belgium, 2023

NOTES ON SOURCES

When Everything's on the Line:
1. 'Elon Musk', Ashlee Vance, p. 65.
2. 'The Red Queen', Matt Ridley, p. 17
3. 'The Black Swan. The Impact of the Highly Improbable', Nassim Nicholas Taleb, prologue, xvii – xviii.

Pillar 1. The Mission Success Equation

Chapter 2:
1. 'Narconomics. How to Run a Drug Cartel', Tom Wainwright. A.o. Value chain data p. 17, 18, 272, 273.
2. 'Escobar. Drugs. Guns. Money. Power' as told by his brother Roberto Escobar, p. 58, 76.

Chapter 3:
1. 'What Is Strategy?' – Michael Porter, HBR, product number 4134.
2. 'Playing To Win. How Strategy Really Works' – A.G. Lafley & Roger L. Martin, p. 3.
3. From 'The Dirt. Confessions of the World's Most Notorious Rock Band', Mötley Crüe.
4. From 'The Gospel According to Luke', Steve Lukather with Paul Rees.
5. 'Punk Rock. An Oral History', John Robb, p. 448.
6. 'Rise and Kill First. The Secret History of Israel's Targeted Assassinations', R. Bergman, p. 549 / 57 & p. 565.
7. 'The Profit Zone. How Strategic Business Design Will Lead You to Tomorrow's Profits', Adrian Slywotzky & David J. Morrison.
8. 'The 48 Laws of Power', Robert Greene, p. 124, 125.
9. 'Why Digital Transformations Fail. The Surprising Disciplines of How to Take Off and Stay Ahead', Tony Saldanha, p. 106 / 107.
10. 'Managing Your Innovation Portfolio', B. Nagji & G. Tuff, Harvard Business Review, May 2012.
11. 'Only the Paranoid Survive. How to Exploit the Crisis Points That Challenge Every Company and Career', Andrew S. Grove, a.o. p.3, 7, 33.
12. Interview with the author, April 14, 2023.

13. IMD Business School has created most of the strategies on this list.
14. From 'Why Don't We Learn from History?', Sir B.H. Liddell Hart, p. 81.
15. From 'Digital Vortex', J. Loucks, J. Macaulay, A. Noronha, M. Wade, as of p. 29.
16. 'The Content Trap', Bharat Anand.
17. 'The Content Trap', Bharat Anand, Chapter 2, 'The Real Problem with Newspapers', p. 7.
18. Learning from IMD course on 'Leading Digital Transformation', February 2020.
19. 'Why Digital Transformations Fail', Tony Saldanha, p. 5.

Chapter 5:
1. 'Captain Scott', Sir Ranulph Fiennes.
2. Interview with the author, October 8, 2020.
3. 'The Content Trap', Bharat Anand, p. 222/223.

Chapter 6:
1. 'Jack. What I've Learned Leading a Great Company and Great People' – Jack Welch (with John A. Byrne), a.o. p. 111.

Chapter 7:
1. 'They Call Me Supermensch', Shep Gordon, Chapter 7.
2. 'Napoleon the Great', Andrew Roberts, p. 755.
3. 'Napoleon the Great', Andrew Roberts, p. 756.
4. Napoleon chapter based on readings of 'Waterloo' by Bernard Cornwell; 'Napoleon', by Vincent Cronin; 'One Hundred Days; Napoleon's Road to Waterloo' by Alan Schom; 'Napoleon' by Johan Op De Beeck; 'Napoleon the Great' by Andrew Roberts; and personal research: a.o. Waterloo battlefield and museum, Dôme des Invalides and war museum, Vienna Museum for Military History, Fontainebleau castle.
5. 'No Mission is Impossible', Michael Bar-Zohar & Nissim Mishal, Chapter 12.
6. 'The Tipping Point', Malcolm Gladwell, p. 163–166.
7. 'Dominion', Tom Holland, p. 56.
8. 'The Tipping Point', Malcolm Gladwell, p. 141.
9. Livy, 'The War with Hannibal', Book XXII.

Chapter 8:
1. Shared by Mr. William Isaacs, Founder & CEO of Dialogos, in a session for Imperial Brands.
2. LinkedIn article, 'What This Top CEO Knows That You Don't: How to Have a Good Fight', Morten T. Hansen, January 26, 2018.
3. 'Start-Up Nation', Dan Senor & Saul Singer.
4. 'The Utility of Force', Sir Rupert Smith, p. 23.

Chapter 9:
1. 'The American Civil War', John Keegan, p. 89/90.
2. 'Call Sign Chaos', General (ret.) Jim Mattis, p. 42/43.
3. 'Hardcore History', Dan Carlin, p. 12.
4. 'Alexander the Great's Art of Strategy', Partha Bose, p. 58.
5. 'On Grand strategy', John Lewis Gaddis.
6. 'Range', David Epstein, p. 102.
7. 'Range', David Epstein, p. 104.

Chapter 10:
1. 'Robert E. Lee', Brian Holden Reid, p. 189.
2. 'Steve Jobs', Walter Isaacson, p. 564.
3. 'The Innovators', Walter Isaacson, p. 195.
4. 'De Zonnekoning', Johan Op De Beeck, p. 530.
5. 'On Bullshit', Harry G. Frankfurt, p. 56.
6. 'The Hard Truth About Innovative Cultures', Gary P. Pisano, Harvard Business Review, p. 61.
7. The 7 Basic Habits of Highly Effective People', Stephen R. Covey, p. 79–88.

A Hard-Won Iron Man Victory:
1. 'Leaders Inside Out. A Navy Seal's Challenge to Successfully Lead, Inspire, And Motivate Yourself and Others Every Day' – CWO Rob Robertson, USN Ret., SEAL, p. 55.

Pillar 2. F.A.Y.U.R.:
F. Fluid Strategy and Execution:
1. The chapter on Napoleon's Russian Campaign is based on reading of: '1812' by Adam Zamoyski, 'Russia Against Napoleon' by Dominic Lieven; 'Napoleon' by Vincent Cronin; 'Napoleon' by Johan Op De Beeck; 'Napoleon the Great' by Andrew Roberts.
2. 'Front Sight focus', David Havens, p. 3.

3. 'Good to Great', Jim Collins, p. 83.
4. 'The Gift of Fear', Gavin De Becker, p. 102–103, 383.
5. 'Military Misfortunes', Eliot A. Cohen & John Gooch, p. 26.

A. Agility:
1. 'Fools Are Everywhere. The Court Jester Around the World', Beatrice C. Otto, p. 112.
2. Story told by a guide during my visit of Fontainebleau castle near Paris (2017).
3. 'Two Lives of Charlemagne', Einhard & Notker the Stammerer, p. 89, 90.
4. A recommended read on the topic: Darrel Rigby, Sarah Elk & Steve Berez, 'Doing Agile Right. Transformation Without Chaos', Harvard Business Review Press, 2020.
5. 'The Speed of Trust', Stephen M.R. Covey, p. 34, 35.
6. 'The Speed of Trust', Stephen M.R. Covey, p. 57.
7. Interview with the author, July 2015.
8. 'Why the Allies Won', Richard Overy, p. 224, 226, 247.
9. 'The Splendid and The Vile', Erik Laron, p. 154
10. Interview with the author, June 2015.

Y. Your Leadership:
1. Interview with the author, 2015.
2. Interview with the author, 2017.
3. 'The Leader's Compass: Set Your Course for Leadership Success', Ed Ruggero & Dennis F. Haley.
4. Image and reference: 'When Violence Is the Answer', Tim Larkin, p. 63–70.

U. Understanding:
1. 'Hooked', Nir Eyal, p. 54.
2. 'Blink', Malcolm Gladwell.

R. Resilience:
1. Interview with Dan Rather, circulated on Facebook February 1, 2023.
2. 'A Survival Guide For Life', Bear Grylls, p. 121.
3. 'Doing Agile Right', Darrell Rigby, Sarah Elk, Steve Berez, p. 73–75.
4. 't Pallieterke, 'Dulce et decorum est pro patria mori', September 13, 2018.
5. 'Man's Search for Meaning', Viktor E. Frankl.

NOTES ON SOURCES

6. Forbes, 'Why Gillette's New Ad Campaign Is Toxic', January 15, 2019.
7. 'Endurance', Alfred Lansing & 'Leadership in Crisis: Ernest Shackleton and the Epic Voyage of the Endurance', HBS case 9-803-127.
8. 'Jungle Soldier', Brian Moynahan.
9. Based on 'Grit', Angela Duckworth.
10. 'Drive', Daniel H. Pink, p. 154.
11. 'Willpower', Roy F. Baumeister & John Tierney, p. 35.
12. 'Willpower', Roy F. Baumeister & John Tierney, p. 131.
13. 'Willpower', Roy F. Baumeister & John Tierney, p. 96.
14. 'Mindset', Carol S. Dweck.
15. The Invention of Nature', Andrea Wulf, p. 185.
16. Interview with the author.
17. 'The Goldmine Effect', Rasmus Ankersen, p. 253.
18. 'Unbeatable Mind', Mark Divine, p. 48
19. 'Strong on Defence', Sanford Strong, p. 35.
20. 'Manage Your Energy, Not Your Time', Tony Schwarz, HBR, October 2007, p. 65.
21. 'Alchemy', Rory Sutherland, p. 21/22.
22. 'Willpower', Roy F. Baumeister & John Tierney, p. 179.
23. 'The Unthinkable', Amanda Ripley, p. 203.
24. 'No Mission Is Impossible', Michael Bar-Zohar & Nissim Mishal, p. 144.
25. 'Letters From a Stoic', Seneca, p. 198.
26. 'The 7 Habits of Highly Effective People', Stephen R. Covey, p. 188–202.
27. 'Survival: Het S.A.S. Handboek' (Dutch version of 'The SAS Survival Handbook'), John Wiseman, p. 19.
28. 'The Splendid and the Vile', Erik Larson, Chapter 36, p. 185.

Pillar 3. Change Management:

Chapter 1:
1. 'The Red Queen', Matt Ridley, p. 17.
2. 'Peter the Great', Robert K. Massie, p. 316.

Chapter 2:
1. The Irish Times, 'Were U2 Making a Joke or Was the Joke on Them?', October 30, 2018.
2. 'Upheaval', Jared Diamond, Chapter 3, p. 101.
3. 'Leaders Make the Future', Bob Johansen, p. xxii.
4. 'Leaders Make the Future', Bob Johansen, p. 8.

Chapter 3:
1. 'Tiny Habits', by BJ Fogg, p. 4.
2. 'Good Habits', Wendy Wood, p. 63.
3. 'The Power of Habit', Charles Duhigg, p. xviii.
4. 'The Power of Habit', Charles Duhigg, p. 19.
5. 'The Power of Habit', Charles Duhigg, p. 20.
6. 'Willpower', Roy F. Baumeister & John Tierney, p. 178.
7. 'The Power of Habit', Charles Duhigg, p. 97, Chapter 4.
8. 'Tiny Habits', by BJ Fogg, p. 5.
9. 'Tiny Habits', by BJ Fogg, p. 12.
10. 'The Siècle Podcast', David H. Montgomery, June 19, 2020.
11. 'Why CMOs Never Last. And What to Do About It', by Kimberly A. Whitler and Neil A. Morgan, July–August 2017.
12. 'Upheaval', Jared Diamond, Chapter 3.
13. 'Change Was Too Fast at P&G; Jager Goes, Pepper Is Reinstalled', Wall Street Journal, June 9, 2000.
14. 'Rockonomics', Alan B. Kreuger, p. 203.
15. 'Why Digital Transformations Fail', Tony Saldanha, p. 48.
16. 'Leading Change. Why Transformation Efforts Fail', John F. Kotter, Harvard Business Review, January 2007.
17. 'Good to Great', Jim Collins, chapter 3, p. 41.

Pillar 4. Supercharged Team:
1. 'Alexander the Great', Robin Lane Fox, p. 389–399.
2. 'The Campaigns of Alexander', Arrian, p. 338.
3. 'The Art of War', Sun Tzu, 'Terrain' Chapter 20.
4. Interview with the author, June 2015.
5. 'Het Bromvliegeffect', Eva Van Den Broek & Tim Den Heijer, p. 191.
6. Interview with the author.
7. 'Drive', Daniel H. Pink, Part 2, p. 207/208.
8. 'Waterloo', Bernard Cromwell, p. 59 & 'Napoleon, Van Keizer tot Mythe', Johan Op De Beeck, p. 623.
9. 'S.A.S. Rogue Heroes', Ben Macintyre, Chapter 1 & 2, p. 5–25.
10. 'Red Team', Micah Zenko, p. xix.
11. 'Red Team', Micah Zenko, p. xi.
12. Story shared in a keynote by Lieven Scheire.

Pillar 5. Pulling It All Together:
1. 'American Icon', Bryce C. Hoffman.

SELECTED BIBLIOGRAPHY

Anand, Bharat, 'The Content Trap. A Strategist's Guide to Digital Change', Random House, 2016.
Ankersen, Rasmus, 'The Goldmine Effect. Crack The Secrets of High Performance', Icon, 2015.
Arrian, 'The Campaigns of Alexander', Penguin Classics, 1971.
Bar-Zohar, Michael & Mishal, Nissim, 'Mossad. The Great Operations of Israel's Secret Service', The Robson Press, 2012.
Bar-Zohar, Michael & Mishal, Nissim, 'No Mission is Impossible. The Death-Defying Missions of the Israeli Special Forces', Ecco, 2015.
Baumeister, Roy F. & Tierney, John, 'Willpower. Recovering the Greatest Human Strength', Penguin, 2001.
Bergman, Ronen, 'Rise and Kill First. The Secret History of Israel's Targeted Assassinations', Random House, 2018.
Bono, 'Surrender. 40 Songs, One Story', Alfred A. Knopf, 2022.
Bose, Partha, 'Alexander the Great's Art of Strategy', Profile Books, 2003.
Bossidy, Larry & Charan, Ram', 'Execution. The Discipline of Getting Things Done', Crown Business, 2002.
Bradley, James, with Powers, Ron, 'Flags of Our Fathers', Bantam, 2006.
Carlin, Dan, 'Hardcore History' (original title: 'The End Is Always Near'), HarperCollins, 2019.
Clark, Alan, 'Barbarossa. The Russian-German Conflict 1941-1945', Phoenix Press, 2000.
Cohen, Eliot A. & Gooch, John, 'Military Misfortunes. The Anatomy of Failure in War', Free Press, 1990.
Collins, James C. ('Jim') & Porras, Jerry I., 'Built to Last. Successful Habits of Visionary Companies', Random House, 2000.
Collins, Jim, 'Good to Great. Why Some Companies Make the Leap... and Others Don't', Random House, 2001.
Collins, Jim & Hansen, Morten T., 'Great by Choice. Uncertainty, Chaos and Luck – Why Some Thrive Despite of It', HarperCollins 2011.
Cornwell, Bernard, 'Waterloo. The History of Four Days, Three Armies and Three Battles', William Collins, 2015.

Covey, Stephen M.R., with Merrill, Rebecca R., 'The Speed of Trust. The One Thing That Changes Everything', Pocket Books, NA.

Covey, Stephen R., 'The 7 Habits of Highly Effective People', Simon & Schuster, 1992.

Cronin, Vincent, 'Napoleon', HarperCollins, 1971.

De Becker, Gavin, 'The Gift of Fear. And Other Signals That Protect Us from Violence', Dell Publishing, 1997.

Diamond, Jared, 'Guns, Germs and Steel. A Short History of Everybody for the Last 13,000 Years', Vintage, 1998.

Diamond, Jared, 'Upheaval. How Nations Cope with Crisis and Change', Allen Lane, 2019.

Divine, Mark, 'Unbeatable Mind. Forge Resiliency and Mental Toughness to Succeed at An Elite Level', self-published, 2015.

Duckworth, Angela, 'Grit. Why Passion and Resilience Are the Secrets to Success', Penguin Random House, 2017.

Duhigg, Charles, 'The Power of Habit. Why We Do What We Do and How to Change', Random House, 2013.

Dweck, Carol S., 'Mindset. The New Psychology of Success. How We Can Learn to Fulfill Our Potential', Ballantine Books, 2016.

Epstein, David, 'Range. Why Generalists Triumph in A Specialized World', Riverhead Books, 2019.

Escobar, Roberto & Fisher, David, 'Escobar. Drugs. Guns. Money. Power', Hodder, 2010.

Eyal Nir, with Hoover, Ryan, 'Hooked. How to Build Habit-Forming Products', Penguin Business, 2019.

Fiennes, Sir Ranulph, 'Captain Scott', Coronet Books, 2003.

Fogg, B.J., 'Tiny Habits. The Small Things That Change Everything', Virgin, 2019.

Frankfurt, Harry G., 'On Bullshit', Princeton University Press, 2005.

Frankl, Viktor E., 'Man's Search for Meaning', Rider, 2008.

Funakoshi, Gichin, 'Karate-dō. My Way of Life', Kodansha International, 1981.

Gadis, John Lewis, 'On Grand Strategy', Penguin, 2018.

George, Bill, 'Authentic Leadership. Rediscovering the Secrets to Creating Lasting Value', Josey-Bass, 2003.

Gladwell, Malcolm, 'The Tipping Point. How Little Things Can Make a Big Difference', Little, Brown & Company, 2000.

Gladwell, Malcolm, 'Blink. The Power of Thinking Without Thinking', Penguin – Allen Lane, 2005.

Gonzales, Laurence, 'Deep Survival. Who Lives, Who Dies, and Why', W.W. Norton, 2017.

Gordon, Shep, 'They Call Me Supermensch. A Backstage Pass to the Amazing Worlds of Film, Food and Rock 'N' Roll', Ecco, 2017.

Greene, Robert, 'The Concise 48 Laws of Power', Profile Books, 2002.

Grove, Andrew S., 'Only the Paranoid Survive. How to Exploit the Crisis Points That Challenge Every Company and Career', Profile Books, 1996.

Grylls, Bear, 'A Survival Guide for Life. How to Achieve Your Goals, Thrive in Adversity and Grow in Character, Corgi Books, 2012.

Grylls, Bear, 'Your Life. Train For It', Bantam Press, 2014.

Hoffman, Bryce C., 'American Icon. Alan Mulally and the Fight to Save Ford Motor Company', Crown Business, 2012.

Isaacson, Walter, 'Steve Jobs', Little, Brown, 2011.

Isaacson, Walter, 'The Innovators. How a Group of Hackers, Geniuses and Geeks Created the Digital Revolution', Simon & Schuster, 2014.

Jenkins, Roy, 'Churchill', Pan, 2001.

Johansen, Bob, 'Leaders Make the Future. Ten New Leadership Skills for an Uncertain World', BK, 2012.

Johnson, Boris, 'The Churchill Factor. How One Man Made History', Hodder, 2015.

Jonasson, Björn, 'The Sayings of The Vikings (Hávamál)', Gudrun, 1992.

Keegan, John, 'The American Civil War', Vintage Books, 2010.

Krueger, Alan B., 'Rockonomics. A Backstage Tour of What the Music Industry Can Teach Us About Economics and Life', Currency, 2019.

Lafley, A.G. & Martin, Roger L., 'Playing to Win. How Strategy Really Works', Harvard Business Review Press, 2013.

Lane Fox, Robin, 'Alexander the Great', Penguin, 1986.

Lansing, Alfred, 'Endurance. The True Story of Shackleton's Incredible Voyage to the Antartic', Phoenix, 2000.

Larkin, Tim, 'When Violence Is the Answer. Learning How to Do What It Takes When Your Life Is at Stake', Back Bay Books, 2018.

Larsen, Erik, 'The Splendid and the Vile. A Saga of Churchill Family and Defiance During the Blitz', William Collins, 2020.

Lendering, Jona, 'Alexander de Grote. De Ondergang van het Perzische Rijk', Athenaeum – Polak & Van Gennep, 2004.

Lewis, Damien, 'Churchill's Secret Warriors. The Explosive True Story of the Special forces Desperadoes of WWII', Quercus, 2014.

Liddell Hart, Sir Basil Henry, 'Why Don't We Learn from History?', Sophron, 2012.

Lieven, Dominic, 'Russia Against Napoleon. The Battle for Europe, 1807 to 1814, Penguin, 2010.

Livy, 'The War with Hannibal', Penguin Classics, 1965.

Loucks, Jeff; Macaulay, James; Noronha, Andy & Wade, Michael, 'Digital Vortex, How Today's Market Leaders Can Beat Disruptive Competitors at Their Own Game', IMD, 2016.
Macintyre, Ben, 'SAS Rogue Heroes', Penguin Random House, 2016.
Mattis, General (ret.) Jim & West, Bing, 'Call Sign Chaos. Learning to Lead', Random House, 2019.
Miles, Richard, 'Carthage Must Be Destroyed. The Rise and Fall of an Ancient Civilization', Penguin, 2011.
Mötley Crüe (with Neil Strauss), 'The Dirt. Confessions of the World's Most Notorious Rock Band', HarperCollins, 2001.
Moynahan, Brian, 'Jungle Soldier. The True Story of Freddy Spencer Chapman', Quercus, 2010.
Onghena-'t Hooft, Olivier, 'Het Noble Purpose Boek', Lannoo Campus, 2019.
Op De Beeck, Johan, 'Napoleon (2). Van Keizer Tot Mythe', Manteau, 2014.
Op De Beeck, Johan, 'De Zonnekoning. Glorie & Schaduw van Lodewijk XIV', Horizon, 2018.
Overy, Richard, 'Russia's War, 1941–1945', Penguin, 2020.
Overy, Richard, 'Why the Allies Won', Pimlico, 2006.
Pink, Daniel H., 'Drive. The Surprising Truth About What Motivates Us', Canongate, 2018.
Polman, Paul & Winston Andrew S., 'Net Positive. How Courageous Companies Thrive by Giving More Than They Take', Harvard Business Review Press, 2021.
Postman, Neil, 'Amusing Ourselves to Death', Penguin, 1985.
Reid, Brian Holden, 'Robert E. Lee. Icon for a Nation', Prometheus Books, 2007.
Richards, Keith, 'Life', Weidenfeld & Nicolson, 2010.
Ridley, Matt, 'The Red Queen. Sex and the Evolution of Human Nature', Penguin, 1994.
Rigby, Darrell, Elk, Sarah & Berez, Steve, 'Doing Agile Right. Transformation Without Chaos', Harvard Business Review Press, 2020.
Ripley, Amanda, 'The Unthinkable. Who Survives When Disaster Strikes – And Why', Arrow Books, 2009.
Roberts, Andrew, 'Napoleon the Great', Allen Lane, 2014.
Roberts, Kevin, 'Lovemarks. The Future Beyond Brands', Powerhouse Books.
Roberts, Kevin, '64 Shots. Leadership in a Crazy World', Powerhouse Books.
Robertson, Rob, 'Leaders Inside Out', self-published, 2018.
Roux, Georges, 'Ancient Iraq', Penguin, 1992.
Ruggero, Ed, & Haley, Dennis F., 'The Leader's Compass: Set Your Course for Leadership Success', Academy Leadership, 2003.

Saldanha, Tony, 'Why Digital Transformations Fail. The Surprising Disciplines of How to Take Off and Stay Ahead', Berrett-Koehler, 2019.

Schom, Alan, 'One Hundred Days', Penguin, 1992.

Senar, Dan & Singer, Saul, 'Start-Up Nation. The Story of Israel's Economic Miracle', Twelve, 2009.

Seneca, Lucius, 'Letters From a Stoic', Penguin Classics, 2004.

Slywotzky, Adrian J. & Morrison, David J., 'The Profit Zone. How Strategic Business Design Will Lead You to Tomorrow's Profits', Times Business – Random House, 1997.

Smith, General (ret.) Sir Rupert, 'The Utility of Force'. The Art of War in the Modern World', Penguin, 2006.

Strong, Sanford, 'Strong on Defense. Survival Rules to Protect You and Your Family from Crime', Pocket Books, 1996.

Sun Tzu, 'The Art of War', Oxford University Press, 1963.

Sutherland, Rory, 'Alchemy. The Surprising Power of Ideas That Don't Make Sense', WH Allen, 2019.

Syed, Matthew, 'Black Box Thinking. Marginal Gains and the Secrets of High Performance', John Murray, 2015.

Taleb, Nassim Nicholas, 'The Black Swan. The Impact of the Highly Improbable', Penguin Allen Lane, 2007.

Thucydides, 'History of the Peloponnesian War', Penguin Classics, 1972.

Treacy, Michael & Wiersema, Fred, 'The Discipline of Market Leaders. Choose Your Customers, Narrow Your Focus, Dominate Your Market', Basic Books, 1995.

Van Den Broek, Eva & Den Heijer, Time, 'Het Bromvliegeffect. Alledaagse fenomenen die stiekem je gedrag sturen', Spectrum, 2021.

Vance, Ashlee, 'Elon Musk. How The Billionaire CEO of SpaceX and Tesla Is Shaping Our Future', Virgin, 2015.

Von Manstein, Erich, 'Lost Victories. The War Memoirs of Hitler's Most Brilliant General', Zenith Press, 2004.

Wainwright, Tom, 'Narconomics. How to Run a Drug Cartel', Penguin Random House, 2016.

Welch, Jack (with John A. Byrne), 'Jack: What I've Learned Leading a Great Company and Great People', Headline, 2001.

Welch, Jack (with Suzy Welch), 'Winning', Harper Business, 2005.

Willink, Jocko & Babin, Leif, 'Extreme Leadership. How U.S. Navy Seals Lead and Win', St. Martin's Press, 2015.

Wiseman, John, 'The SAS Survival Handbook' / 'Survival: Het S.A.S. Handboek', Dutch version: Zomer & Keuning, 1988.

Wood, Wendy, 'Good Habits, Bad Habits. The Science of Making Positive Changes That Stick', MacMillan, 2019.

Xenophon, 'The Persian Expedition', Penguin Classics, 1972.

Zamoyski, Adam, '1812. Napoleon's Fatal March on Moscow', Harper Perennial, 2005.

Zenko, Micah, 'Red Team. How To Succeed by Thinking Like the Enemy', Basic Books, 2015.

INDEX

Adams, Douglas 272
   The Hitchhiker's Guide to the Galaxy 272
Aeschylus 137
Agility 157, 167, 176, 284
   A definition of Agility 167
   Agile innovation 170
   Agility towards others 173
   Bureaucracy 176
   Change agility 173
   Develop Learning Agility 172
   Jesters case studies 167
   Mental agility 173
   Minimum Viable Products 170
   Results agility 173
   Self-awareness 173
   Simplify 173
   Trust 171
Akbar the Great 167
Alcoa Corporation 237
   O'Neill, Paul 237
Alcoholics Anonymous 232
Alderfeld, Gustavus 159
Alexander I, Tsar 151
Alexander the Great 130, 259
Allen, Mark 195
American Civil War 122, 136
Amundsen, Roald 85, 88
Anand, Bharat 71
Ancien Regimen 232
Ankersen, Rasmus 207

Anthrax 194
Antonov, Aleksei 214
Anvil 194
Apple 64, 65, 70
   iPod 64, 65, 70
   iTunes 64, 65
Armstrong, Neil 92
Arrian 130, 259
Artifical Intelligence 23, 65
Atahuallpa 222
Axel Springer 72
Bain Consulting 123
Barak, Ehud 103
Barclay de Tolly, Mikhail 152
Battle of Gettysburg 136
Beats Electronics 65, 68
Becht, Bart 115
Bergh, Chip 93, 253, 261
Bezos, Jeff 249
Birbal 167
Black Swans 23
Blitzkrieg 164
Blücher, Gebhard Leberecht 100
Bolt, Usain 200
Boomy 65
Boothe Luce, Claire 200
Bowie, David 223, 271
   Aladdin Sane 223
   Ashes to Ashes 223
   Let's Dance 223
   Life on Mars? 271

The Thin White Duke   223
Ziggy Stardust   223
Briant, Aristide   69
British Airways   52
Burnett, Leo   93
Caesar, Julius   130, 156
Capabilities   20, 21, 76, 121, 144, 171, 270
   Analogical thinking   131, 132
   Competence leads to confidence   124
   Employee and leader responsibility   128
   In depth or on a wider front   122
   Inspiration   127
   Leaders must be readers   121, 128
   Learning Plans   121, 124
   Mastery   124, 265
   Means and capabilities   121
   Microbattles   121, 123, 245
   Story telling   133
Caroll, Lewis   23
Carroll, Lewis
   Alice in Wonderland   23, 221
   Through the Looking Glass   23
Challagalla, Gautham   59
Change Management   20, 23, 219, 276
   Acceptance that change is needed   232
   Anticipating change   224
   Barriers and insights   239
   Change management process   232
   Change starts with a decision   232
   Creative destruction   23, 222
   Early wins   106, 244, 246
   Emotion and psychology   252
   Evolution   21, 253
   Evolutionary approach   227
   Get on the bus   251
   Guiding coalition   250
   Habits   210, 235, 258
   How   231
   Innovator's dilemma   224
   Keystone habit   235, 237, 263
   Most only move when a crisis hits   226
   Overcommunicate   93, 253
   People changes   253
   Reactive response   225
   Reasons for resistance   232
   Revolution   66, 227, 232
   Right timing   228
   Sigmoid curve   224
   Stakeholder mapping   242
   The Red Queen   23, 221
   The Tiny Habits Method   238
   Topical or structural   247
   What to keep, pace change   249
   When   223
   Why   221
Chang Yü   260
Charlemagne   167
Charles XII   159
Christensen, Clayton   224
Christiaens, Denis   180
Churchill, Winston   175, 227, 246, 268
Citrin, Jim   205
Colgate   36
Collins, Jim   155, 251
Cooper, Alice   97
Covey, Stephen M.R.   171
Covey, Stephen R.   141
Covid-19   23
Crosby, Stills & Nash   40
Dansercour, Dixie   86, 88, 102
Danziger, Shai   202
Dayan, General Moshe   180
De Beers   55

Dedrijvere, Philiep   172
Deloitte   75
De Rebecque, General Baron Jean Victor Constant   266
Diamond, Jared   222
Dilbert   271
Divine, Mark   208
Dr. Dre   64, 65
Dr. Seuss   194
Drucker, Peter   130, 258
Duckworth, Angela   199
Duke of Wellington   100, 266
Dumb and Dumber   69
Duncker, Karl   131
Dweck, Dr. Carol S.   203
EasyJet   53
Edmondson, Amy   270
Eli Lilly   60
Endel   65
Escobar, Pablo   41, 45
Escobar, Roberto   45
F.A.Y.U.R.   20, 22, 149, 247, 276
  Agility   167
  Fluid Strategy and Execution   151
  Resilience   193
  Understanding   187
  Your Leadership   179
Fiennes, Sir Ranulph   85
Figures
  1. The 4 Pillars of Mission Success   24
  2. The Lean Organism Management Model   25, 274
  3. The Moroccan Paradox   43
  4. The Digital Vortex   71
  6. Choice Cascading   75
  7. The OGSM   77
  8. The Gillette Go-to-Market Model   84
  9. The Message Track   94
  10. The CBA Loop   111
  11. The Unity and Good Fight Model   116
  12. Strategy Into Action - 5 Critical Factors   117
  13. Microbattle Mapping   123
  15. The Accountability Matrix   139
  16. The Ownership Matrix   140
  17. Circle of Concern / Circle of Influence   141
  18. The Mission Success Equation   147
  19. Tactics - Critical Factors   162
  20. The Agility Triangle   170
  21. Energy Management   206
  22. The Change Cycle & The Sigmoid Curve   224
  23. The Habit Loop   236
  24. Barriers and Insights Applied to a Change Program   241
  25. Stakeholder Mapping   242
  26. The Action Plan   275
Fillmore, Millard   226
Fluid Strategy and Execution   151
  Adapting to the present   161
  A definition of Tactics   162
  Anticipating the future   160
  Be pro-active   164
  Competition has a vote   153
  Dare to retreat   158
  Deception   107, 163
  Frontline operational freedom   165
  Go and See   181, 228
  LEAN   161
  Learning from failure   159
  Learning from the past   160
  Napoleon Russia case study   151
  OPSEC   162

Practice contingency planning 154
Reserve 156
Resource agility 156
RICE test 156
Stockdale Paradox 155
Sunk cost fallacy 158
Surprise 162
Tactical capability 162
Understand the psychology 164
Unity of doctrine 165
FN Meka 66
Fogg, B.J. 238
Ford 221, 276
Formula 1 76
Frankfurt, Dr. Harry 137
Frankl, Victor 196
Friedman, Thomas 172
Gaddis, John Lewis 131
Gat, Colonel Sharon 182
Gaza 53
General Motors 276
Gillette 57, 81, 82, 85, 111, 121, 198, 233, 252, 264, 265
   Blue 3 234
   Disposables 82
   Fusion 83, 233
   Mach 3 233
   Point of Market Entry programs 112
   The CDI wheel 83
   The gifting season 83
Gladwell, Malcolm 104, 191
Google 63, 65
   Schmidt, Eric 63
Gorbachev, Mikhail 78, 215
Gordon, Shep 97, 282
Grisham, John 194
Grove, Andrew S. 63, 136
Grylls, Bear 193

Guderian, Heinz 214
Hannibal 97, 107
   Cannae 108
   Carthage 107
   Maharbal, cavalry commander 108
Hansen, Morten T. 116
Harvard Business Review 49, 63, 247, 250
Havens, David 155
Henley, William Ernest 216
Henri II 167
Herremans, Marc 143, 144, 145
   To Walk Again 145
Hitler, Adolf 213
Hollywood 91
Honda 92
H.R.M. King Mohamed VI 38
Iovine, Jimmy 65
   Interscope Records 65
Iron Man 143, 144, 145
Israel 53, 94, 102, 113, 116, 270
   Start-Up Nation 116
Israeli Airforce 114
Iwo Jima 216
Jager, Durk I. 113, 249
Japan 67, 226, 248, 249, 250
   Samurai 21, 226
   The Meiji restoration 227
   Tokugawa shogun 226
Jobs, Steve 136
Johansen, Bob 228
Kadri, Ilham 271
Karate 21, 194, 208, 263
   Funakoshi, Gichin 263
Keller, Helen 141
Kelling, George 105
Kennedy, John F. 92, 200
Keynes, John Maynard 269
Khan, Praga 66

Lords of Acid 66
King, Martin Luther 92
Kotter, John P. 250
Kovic, Ron 146
Krav Maga 20, 120
Kutuzov, Mikhail 153, 157, 164
Lafferty, James Michael 67
Lafley, A.G. 57, 249
Laundry detergent
    Game of inches 161
    Hand-wash 34
    Machine-wash 33
    Polybags 34, 79
    Suds 33, 79, 187, 247
Layforce 267
Lee, Robert E. 136
Leipzig, Adam 209
Levav, Jonathan 202
Lichtenstein, Roy 132
Lincoln, Abraham 122
Lithuania 151
Livy 108, 130
L'Oreal 36
Louis XIV 136
Lukather, Steve 50
Lydon, John 52
Machiavelli, Niccolo 131
Maffletone, Dr. Phil 195
Mandela, Nelson 216
Mattis, General (ret.) James N. 128
McCullough, Michael 210
McDonald, Robert A. 127, 135, 262
McDonalds 59
McKinsey 247
Medal of Honor 21
Megadeth 194
Metallica 64, 194
Meyer, Claude L. 181, 191
Microsoft 58
Monitor 75

Mötley Crüe 50
Mulally, Alan 276
Musk, Elon 21, 194, 271
    SpaceX 21, 271
Napoleon 97, 99, 100, 130, 151, 153, 156, 158, 159, 164, 244, 245
    Austerlitz 152
    Borodino 153, 156
    Friedland 152
    Imperial Guard 99, 156
    Ligny 100
    Moscow 153, 156
    Quatre Bras 100, 266
    Smolensk 153, 165
    Treaty of Erfurt 152
    Treaty of Tilsit 152
    Waterloo 99, 244, 266
Napster 64, 65
Navy SEALs 119, 172, 263
Nazi Germany 173, 214
Netanyahu, Benjamin 'Bibi' 103
Netflix 70
Ney, Michel 100, 266
Nietzsche, Friedrich 193, 196
No Excuse Ownership 20, 21, 135, 144, 165, 276
    Accountability 139
    Circle of concern 142
    Circle of influence 141
    Decision rights 139, 165, 247
    Leaders must demonstrate no excuse ownership 136
    Ownership matrix 140
    Part of the culture 138
    The Circle of Influence 135
    The Ownership Matrix 135
    Truth 138
    Truth and clear language 136
Notker the Stammerer 167
Oasis 50

Oates, Lawrence 'Titus'   88
Ohno, Taiichi   188
Paullus   107
Peace Treaty of Versailles   70
Pepper, John E.   39, 249
Perfect Execution   20, 21, 97, 145, 275
   AAR (After Action Review)   111, 114, 115, 160
   A definition of Execution   98
   A definition of Tactics   98
   At the time of execution, act with conviction   119
   Broken windows theory   105
   CBA (Current Best Approach)   111, 112, 113, 119
   Dichotomy strategy / execution   109
   Explain the why   119
   Factors impacting outcomes   104
   Flawed execution   99
   Hannibal case study   107
   McLaren   102
   Never get into something unless you can sustain it   117
   Operation White Angels   102, 212
   Positive conflict   114, 115
   Practical Ways to Improve Execution   111
   Process to drive executional excellence   118
   Six Sigma   118
   Social context   105
   Sweat the small stuff   102
   Tactically sound, strategically weak   107
   The Good Samaritan case study   104
   Waterloo case study   99

Peter the Great   159
P&G   113, 117, 135, 162, 174, 175, 181, 191, 249, 252, 264
   CEEMEA   80, 82, 121, 233, 252, 264
   Folgers   241
   Poland   34, 42
   Vicks VapoRub   241
P&G Morocco   31, 41, 56, 61, 75, 78, 95, 106, 118, 127, 162, 180, 185, 187, 189, 201, 238, 242, 245, 258, 262, 265, 276
   Ace   34
   Always   34, 42, 79
   Ariel   34, 189
   Barriers to entry   56
   Bonux   185
   Casablanca   37, 127, 195
   Change Management   251
   Competition   35
   Comunivers   36, 79, 250
   First moment of truth   80
   Flower Power   262
   Free trade   56, 62
   Free trade agreements   39
   From Darkness to Light   75, 78, 95
   Hair Care   34, 43, 79
   Hot Chocolate   262
   In Search of Excellence   118
   Internal Controls   32, 80
   Investment agreement   39, 61, 243
   Knowledge Miles   126, 245
   Marketing   35
   Mission Itspossible   78, 95, 245
   Mr. Propre   35
   OGSM   78
   Pacing the change   250
   Pampers   34, 39, 42, 61, 79
   Rural   35, 38, 39, 56, 79

September 11   195, 243
The landscape   38
The Moroccan Paradox   42, 247
The organization   36
The portfolio   32
The trade   38
Tide   32, 33, 36, 61, 79, 185, 187, 189, 239, 246, 248
U.F.O. Maroc   127, 246
Unions   40, 243
Philip Morris International   66
   IQOS   67
   Marlboro   67
Pisano, Gary P.   138
Pizarro González, Francisco   222
Polman, Paul   175, 179, 260
Porsche   53
Porter, Michael E.   49, 75
Queen   265
Reagan, Ronald   78, 215
Reckitt-Benckiser   115
Red Team   270
Rescorla, Rick   211
Resilience   193
   A definition of Purpose   196
   A definition of Resilience   193
   Adversity as source of strength   193
   Build 'Grit' & Willpower   198
   Energy Management   205
   Fixed mindset   203
   Get purpose   196
   Growth mindset   203
   Heroes, songs, poems, visuals   216
   Israeli parole case study   202
   Keep the focus external   213
   Mindsetting   208
   Muscle memory   209, 210, 211, 212

Perseverance   200
   The emotional bank account   213
   The Never Give Up Club   193
   The secret of grit   199
Ribot, Alexandre-Felix-Joseph   69
Ridley, Matt   23, 221
Roberts, Kevin   94, 127
Robertson, Rob   146
Robespierre, Maximilien   227
Rome   107
Rosenthal, Joe   216
Russia   151
Sadhguru   124
Saint Paul   231
   Epiphany   231
   Saul of Tarsus   231
SAS   193, 215, 268, 269
Schumpeter, Joseph   222
Schwarz, Tony   209
Scott, Robert Falcon   85
Seneca   130, 141, 212
Sense of humor   215
September 11   195, 211, 225, 243
Shackleton, Ernest   87, 198
Sheikh Yassin   53
Silicon Valley   170
SKU   109, 173, 174
Slayer   194
Slywotzky & Morrison   57
Smith, General (ret.) Sir Rupert   117
Socratic dialogue   189
Sony   64
South Pole   85
Soviet Union   173
Sparta   109, 129
Special Forces   161, 182, 193, 206, 268
Spencer Chapman, Freddy   199
Spinoza, Baruch   179
Spotify   65

Stalin, Joseph   131, 196, 213
Stanley, Paul   193
Steele Lewes, Lieutenant John   269
Stirling, Lieutenant Archibald David   267
Stockdale, Admiral Jim   155
Stockdale Paradox   155
Stoicism   197
Strategic Clarity   20, 21, 31, 91, 144, 274
  A definition of Go-to-Market Models   82
  A definition of Strategy   49
  Barriers to entry   54, 126
    De Beers case study   55
  Brand Value   59
  Bring it alive, everywhere   95
  Choice Cascading   75
  Choices   49, 69, 76, 78, 80, 112, 119, 133
  Considerations When Developing Strategy   49
  Core business   59, 63, 153, 174, 198
  Digital   23, 64, 65, 66, 113, 124, 250
    newspaper case study   71
  Digital is an enabler   70
  Digital transformation   72
  Do not overcomplicate things   94
  Ego   69
  Elevator speech   93
  Game changer   64, 68, 78
  Go-to-Market Models   59, 82, 85, 88, 233, 234, 274
    Gillette case study   82
    South Pole case study   85
    Walmart case study   89
  Go-to-Market Models cannot be blindly copied   89

Hope is not a strategy   69
Inspirational language   92
Key drivers of profit   59
KPIs   78, 125, 140, 237
Magic goal   92
Message track   93
Miller's Law   94
Music industry   224
  game changers   64
  The Sea of Poppies case study   51
  U2 case study   51
OGSM   77, 80, 140, 245, 274
Options to defend against a game changer   68
Overcommunicate   93
Pharmaceutical industry   60
prework   41
  external consultant   47
  input from employees on the frontline   47
Prework
  Assess the landscape   41
  Assess the organization   44
  drug cartel case study   44
  Review the Competition   44
  SWOT analysis   44
  Understand the profit model   42
Profit model   46, 59, 72
Profit zone
  Customer Selection   57
  strategic control points   58
  Value Capture   58
Set the strategic scene   60
Straddling   49, 52
Strategic control points   57, 58
Strategic inflection point   63, 66
Strategy expressed in a metaphor   91

The P&G Morocco case study   31
The Power of One Dollar   91
The profit model   42, 51, 71
Tobacco industry   66, 67, 68
Unintended consequences   53, 261
Sun Tzu   107, 130, 157, 164, 260
Supercharged Team   20, 24, 257, 276
   Add some rock & roll   271
   A definition of Culture   258
   Diversity of the mind   266
   Focus on culture   258
   Intrinsic motivation   265
   Management by walking around   271
   Manage the context   266
   Mavericks   266
   Promotion policy   263
   Rituals   263
   SAS case study   267
   Six drivers of culture   258
   The reward system   261
   Tone from the top   259
Sutherland, Rory   269
Tennyson, Lord Alfred   88
Terrorism
   Erez border attack   53
   Hamas   53
   London, June 3, 2017   20
   Operation White Angels   102
   September 11, 2001   195, 211
The 4 Pillars of Mission Success   19
The Beatles   182, 183, 194
   Best, Pete   182
   Epstein, Brian   182
   Harrison, George   182
   Lennon, John   182
   McCartney, Paul   182
   Revolver   182
   Sgt. Peppers   182

   Starr, Ringo   182
The Clash   184
   Headon, 'Topper'   184
   London Calling   184
   Strummer, Joe   184
The Kinks   50, 127
   Davies, Ray   50
The Lean Organism Management Model   20, 25, 110, 273
   Action Plan   140, 275
   The Action Room   276
The Mission Success Equation   20, 21, 22, 29, 143, 146, 165, 172, 182, 247
The Rolling Stones   182
   Jagger, Mick   183
   Loog Oldham, Andrew   183
   Richards, Keith   183
   Stewart, Ian 'Stu'   183
The The   197
The Who   127
Thucydides   109
Tintin   127
Tolstoy, Leo   131
Tyson, Mike   154
U2   51, 52, 182, 183, 225, 285
   Achtung Baby   225
   All That You Can't Leave Behind   225
   Clayton, Adam   184
   McGuinness, Paul   52
   Pop   225
   PopMart   225
   Rattle and Hum   225
   The Joshua Tree   225
Understanding   187
   Compulsory 'in touch' program   188
   Ensure continuity   190
   Intellectual democracy   190

Manage by asking questions 189
The 5 Why's Method 188
The why 119, 188
Unilever 34, 35, 44, 80, 112, 173, 175, 179, 206
   Omo 34, 35, 44, 187, 239, 246
   Sunsilk 36
Van Halen, Eddie 254
Varro 107
Virchow, Rudolf 60
Voltaire 159
Volvo 266
Von Bismarck, Otto 60, 129
Von Clausewitz, Carl 131
Von Koenigswald, Gustav Heinrich Ralph 261
Von Manstein, Erich 214
Von Moltke, Helmuth 154
VUCA 23, 102, 129, 146, 172, 183, 184

Walmart 89
Welch, Jack 92, 249
West Point 135, 264
   Cadet's Prayer 179
Wilson, James Q. 105
Xenophon 130
Your Leadership 19, 179
   Acknowledge mistakes 185
   Build 'heart' 182
   Harder right versus easier wrong 179
   Leader's compass 184
   Leadership from the front 180
   Lhe line of command 181
   Sum bigger than individual parts 182
   The line of communication 181
Ze'evi, General Revaham 103
Zenko, Micah 270
Zhukov, Georgy 214

Ghent, Belgium
info@owlpress.be
www.owlpress.be

ISBN 9789072201836
NUR 801
Thema KJMB
D2023/11.089/119
© 2023, Borgerhoff & Lamberigts nv

Authors: Peter Corijn

Coordination: Sophie Vanluchene, Nina Waegemans, Paulien Vandenberghe, Joni Verhulst
Copy-editor: Karoline Segers
Proofreader: Ali March
Cover design: Bart Luijten
Design lay-out: Robin J. August
Typesetting: Crius Group

Printed in Europe

First published in September 2023

No part of this publication may be reproduced and/or made public by means of print, photocopy, electronic medium or by any other means, without prior written permission from the publisher.

In compiling this publication, the publisher has tried to contact and credit all copyright holders. Should there be a recording without prior knowledge of the copyright holder, we request to please contact the publisher.